Flying
N(
20₁ ⁊

Managing Editor: Steve Lindahl

Poetry Editor: Angell Caudill

Non-fiction Editor: Jennifer Stevenson Vincent

Fiction Editor: Ray Morrison

Fiction Readers: Bob Shar
                       Steve Lindahl

President's Favorite chosen by:
                       Bart Ganzert

Cover Art: Barbara Rizza Mellin

Flying South is a literary magazine/writing contest published annually by Winston-Salem Writers, an association of writers and readers with the purpose of:

Helping writers interact with other writers, improve their craft, and realize their goals.

Information about Winston-Salem Writers can be found at the website: **www.wswriters.org**

Winston-Salem Writers is a non-profit organization and a member of The Arts Council of Winston-Salem and Forsyth County, NC.

Contents

2019 Best in Category Winners:

Non-Fiction:

Fiction:

Poetry:

Pamela Akins

Some Things Can't Be Fixed

On the first day of a ten-day tour of Israel, my husband and I passed the skeleton of the Dolphinarium Discotheque, its torn walls an eyesore among swanky hotels along the Tel Aviv beachfront. At a distance, I'd thought it might have some archeological significance. But when we got closer, its gray concrete and garish graffiti told me it was no timeworn ruin.

"Why do you think such prime real estate has been left undeveloped?" I said.

My husband shrugged. "Odd, with all the high-rise hotels here."

We put it behind us, intent on seeing what the Holy Land was really like.

The site remained a mystery, the broken concrete forgotten, as we traveled the country. Then by chance, on the next to last day of our trip, we shared a taxi with an American engineer from Minnesota who worked for a nonprofit, managing development projects in the West Bank. He told us he had lived in Ramallah for several years and was back in Israel to develop plans for repairing a well in Jaffa; the well was a major water source for that ancient, mostly-Arab city just south of Tel Aviv. He pointed to the derelict structure and said, "Did you see the Dolphinarium?"

"The what?" I said.

"The Dolphinarium. After the dolphins left, it became a discotheque, a popular beach hangout. Or, it was until a Second Intifada suicide bomber killed twenty-one people there."

"Twenty-one?"

"Yeah, and most of them were teenagers. The Israelis leave it like that to remind everyone that they are constantly under threat."

My husband and I remained silent as we'd done so many other times on this trip. What could we say? It seemed strange to leave a monument to death and destruction in such a beautiful place. But by then we were well-versed in the history of Israel in Palestine and the Israeli mindset that came with their fight for survival in a land of perpetual conflict.

We'd come to Israel as part of a Jewish Federation tour. Our friend Jerry was the executive director of the local Federation and was known for leading personalized ecumenical trips there. He'd been asking us to join him for years. As a mixed marriage couple— my husband was Jewish and I was raised Southern Baptist—we'd avoided the trip. Israel was at the heart of our differences; it was easier not to confront them. We'd lived our thirty-plus years of married life in between, sharing a little of this and a little of that, but never answering the hard questions. Ambiguity was what love demanded.

But we couldn't put Jerry off any longer—he was just too persuasive. He suggested we join him on a trip he was making to a worldwide gathering of Jewish Federations. We'd get the benefit of a structured tour for the first few days. Then he'd take us to Galilee to see traditional Christian sights and show us around Jerusalem before we struck out on our own.

Throughout the trip, the signs of an uneasy peace were all around us. At the beginning, our Israeli tour guide, Lev, talked about serving as a tank commander in the Israeli Defense Force (IDF), explaining that every Israeli citizen must serve in the military—all, that is, except for the ultra-orthodox Jewish men who spend their days studying the Torah. He also explained that many secular Israelis were fed up with this system where the very religious didn't pay their fair share of taxes and weren't required to put in two years of military duty. As Americans, we all agreed: everyone should pay their fair share and serve.

When we visited an IDF post in the Golan Heights, young uniformed men and women gave us a demonstration of their marksmanship, firing off AK-47 rounds at targets in a rock-strewn field. We held our hands over our ears while the air filled with "pop, pop, pop," a metallic smell assailed our nostrils, and spent shells fell at our feet. I picked up a warm shell, thinking I'd keep it as a souvenir, but was told to leave it where it fell. I let it drop.

Afterwards, we were taken to a compound where the soldiers lived and trained, high on a hill overlooking the Syrian border. Slate-green hills mounded toward the northeast beneath blue skies and white cumulus clouds. The soldiers lined up in the courtyard of their Mediterranean-styled barracks with its arches and columns and showed off their weaponry and gear, while the commander explained the rough-terrain training they endured. A petite young woman in brown khakis, auburn ponytail and bright smile showed us night-vision and sighting pieces.

Off to the side, another soldier stood alert next to a white column. He looked like a dark clown at a Mardi Gras party: He wore a loose-fitting camouflage field uniform. A long-muzzled gun hung over his shoulder and down his right side. On his head, a dark green and brown *mitznefet*, like a large chef's hat, flopped down over his right ear and hung against the back of his neck. His skin was blackened from neck to hairline. His eyes, small pools of white with dark irises, watched over us, his red lips a grim slash across the black shadow of his face. While the others were light and friendly, he never stepped outside his life-and-death stance.

"What kind of threat do you face here?" one of the Americans asked.

"Every now and then, we get shots fired into Israel from Syria," the commander said. "But we're more concerned about Hezbollah terrorists sneaking across the border when it's dark. We have patrols out there every night."

A slight murmur arose from the Americans. We could see those far off hills and the rocky terrain in between. The black-faced soldier standing silently to the side seemed less clownish.

Then the Israeli commander proudly introduced a young man from California who had made *aliyah*—returned to the Jewish homeland—and enlisted in the Israeli military. The kid beamed at his fellow Americans, his cheeks sunburned, his close-cropped reddish hair covered by a brown Golani Brigade beret. I didn't understand why American parents would encourage their sons or daughters to enlist in the military of a foreign country, especially one where the threat of war was so present. But most of our fellow tourists nodded in approval—another Jew coming home. "Next year in Jerusalem," they'd said at Passover.

After the demonstration, some of the Americans— mostly the men—held an AK-47 for pictures. Jerry happily posed with the gun, while my husband gingerly hung it over his shoulders and grinned sheepishly for the camera. I'd heard his stories about being an unhappy Marine reservist and the extra grief he got in boot camp for being a soft Jew-boy trying to avoid Vietnam. The black gun looked out of place against his coral Columbia travel shirt.

A few days later, after we'd broken away from the Jewish Federation tour, my husband and I passed through armed checkpoints into the West Bank to visit Masada, the hilltop fortress where Jewish zealots fled after Romans destroyed the Second Temple. The zealots have been venerated as heroes for millennia, symbols of Jewish freedom in their own land. Rather than be taken captive, they killed their women and children before committing suicide.

We wandered about the broad hilltop, exploring the remnants of King Herod's summer palace and the zealots' fortifications. My husband was fascinated by the dirt ramp the Romans built to attack the Jewish fighters. I was more interested in finding the cisterns where, according to Jewish historian Flavius Josephus, two women and five children hid from the suicidal assault and survived to tell the story of Masada.

From atop the fortress plateau, we could see the Dead Sea to the east—a long slice of gray-blue water fringed by white salt deposits. Our guide pointed out industrial operations by the Israelis and Jordanians to extract potash, salt and bromine. He also noted the sea was shrinking because of diversion of the River Jordan and the salt mining operations.

Even our side trip to the resort town of Eilat, Israel's port sandwiched between Jordan and Saudi Arabia at the northern tip of the Red Sea, was peppered with reminders of threat. During the hour ride from Jerusalem to the small airport in Tel Aviv, our taxi driver told us about being shot at by Palestinian snipers hiding in the hills along the roadside. Before our flight, I was asked to open my luggage. My tour books had appeared as solid shadows on security screens—hollowed-out books can conceal bombs.

Then, while in Eilat, we watched a standoff between an Israeli police boat and a fishing boat that had wandered over from the adjacent port of Aqaba. For about thirty minutes, the police broadcast threats in multiple languages, including English, telling the fishing boat, "Please Leave Israeli Waters. Now." Swimmers left the water and sunbathers gathered their towels and returned to their hotel rooms to watch the standoff from balconies. In the end, the fishermen, if that's what they were, returned to Jordanian territory, and the vacationers returned to the beach.

The day we toured Bethlehem and East Jerusalem with a private guide was the most telling. We met Dani downstairs in the hotel foyer. He wore jeans, a light blue shirt, a black jacket, and dark sunglasses. His shoulder-length black hair was slicked back from his forehead in a neat ponytail at the base of his neck. A narrow aquiline nose dominated his face.

Dani removed his sunglasses and shook our hands. "May I ask your religion?"

My husband and I looked at each other. Religion was the essence of Jerusalem, but we were still surprised at the question.

"Why do you ask?" my husband said. Even as an American Jew, he'd learned to be cautious.

Dani adjusted his stance. "Because I tailor my tours to my customers' religion."

Unsure how to explain our complicated relationship, we told him what we'd already seen—Via Dolorosa, the Wailing Wall and Jewish Quarter, the Muslim Quarter and souk, the Church of the Holy Sepulchre. He nodded.

Afraid he'd think there wasn't anything new he could show

us, I said, "I want to see Bethlehem."

Dani took us to Bethlehem by way of another armed checkpoint. Once in the West Bank, we stopped to view a famous Banksy drawing and other graffiti decrying the twenty-five-foot concrete barrier that separates Palestinians from Israelis. He showed us where the Aida refugee camp crowded up against the wall and where Palestinians had been shot trying to climb over it. We looked on in neutrality; we'd already heard from our Israeli Jewish guide how the wall had all but stopped random suicide bombings.

In Bethlehem, after seeing the Church of the Nativity, we bought olivewood Christmas ornaments for my family in Texas and a rosary for a Catholic friend in Connecticut.

When we were done shopping, Dani offered us Taybeh beer. "The brewers are friends of mine."

"Oh," I said. I knew the brewery, founded by a Harvard-educated Palestinian Christian, had been heralded as an example of efforts to build connections between Israelis and Palestinians.

My husband shook his head. It was a chilly morning and we weren't big beer drinkers. Following Dani back to the car, I regretted not buying a bottle. The brewery had been doing well until the Israelis put up the wall. Now it was much harder for them to ship their beer into Israel. And the West Bank is not an ideal place for beer sales—Muslims aren't supposed to drink alcohol. I wished I'd done my part for peace.

Outside Bethlehem, Dani drove us to Shepherds' Field, a place of rocky outcrops, an old archeological excavation, and a stone Franciscan chapel.

"Tradition says this is where the angels announced the birth of the Christ child to the shepherds," Dani said. I heard all those Christmas songs I love to sing.

Dani excused himself and went back to the car for a smoke. We wandered around the site and checked out a cave used as a small chapel, its low-hanging ceiling blackened with soot. A busload of smiling Korean Christians filled the Catholic chapel.

After a short while, Dani returned to collect us. He nodded across the arid hills toward a cluster of white apartment towers rising in the middle of nowhere. "That's one of the largest Israeli settlements in the West Bank."

"Palestinian land?" I asked. He nodded. A dry wind blew through the cedars behind us. We looked on and said nothing. We were merely witnesses to broken covenants, old and new.

For lunch, Dani took us back to Jerusalem to a large open-air restaurant in the Armenian section. He knew the owners of the restaurant and ordered for us. Lunch was plentiful and fresh—huge trays of grilled vegetables, roasted rosemary chicken, parsley-and-olive-oil-dressed couscous, and the best lemon hummus I've ever had.

While we ate, Dani told us that, even though he was Christian, he lived in the Jewish section of Jerusalem and sent his children to Jewish schools because he wanted them to do well in Israel. He also told us he had courted a daughter of the restaurant owner and had once been caught in the Armenian section when the gates closed at night. He smiled and told us how the girl's brothers helped him climb over the wall.

"Did you marry her?" my husband asked.

"No." He shook his head. "I'm not Armenian."

"But you're Christian," I said.

"I'm not Armenian," he said. That was that.

After lunch, we toured Mount Zion, visiting traditional Christian sites, such as the Room of the Last Supper, as well as the Jewish Tomb of King David (with its separate access for women). Afterwards, we went to the Mount of Olives, home of the Garden of Gethsemane, the Russian Orthodox Church of Mary Magdalene, and the small octagonal Dome of the Ascension venerated by Jews, Christians and Muslims.

Then we walked along the roadside railing above Kidron Valley and watched the sun set over Jerusalem. Below lay the valley's three-thousand-year-old Jewish cemetery. Black-clad Hasidic Jews walked single-file up a white-tomb-lined path. Their wide-brimmed hats, stark in a sea of pale headstones, cast long shadows along the cemetery trail.

Dani pointed to another cemetery across the valley that climbed the western slope to Jerusalem's grand Golden Gate. "That is where Jesus entered Jerusalem on Palm Sunday, riding a white donkey and fulfilling the prophecy of the coming of the Messiah," he said.

I wasn't sure my husband understood the significance of Palm Sunday, especially since his Messiah had not yet arrived on this earth. I made a mental note to explain later.

When neither of us commented, Dani continued, "Suleiman the Magnificent sealed The Golden Gate about five hundred years ago. Soon after, Muslims began burying their dead in the approach to the gate. Some Jews say it was to block the Prophet Elijah."

"I don't understand," I said.

"Cemeteries are off-limits to Jewish priests," Dani said. "As long as the Muslim cemetery is there, Elijah can't pass through the Golden Gate into Jerusalem and announce the Messiah."

Checkmate, I thought. My husband's Messiah could never come.

Above the gate, the sun's last rays gleamed off the golden Dome of the Rock on the Temple Mount. We already knew the Mount had been the site of the Jews' Second Temple and the Muslim shrine was built over six hundred years after the Temple was destroyed. Dani explained that the Dome of the Rock enshrined the Foundation Stone where, according to Muslim belief, Mohammed ascended into heaven.

But reverence for the Foundation Stone is older than Islam. Jews believe the Foundation Stone is where Abraham offered Isaac, his first-born son, in sacrifice and was stopped by an angel. Some believe the Foundation Stone is where the Ark of the Covenant sat within the Temple's Holy of Holies. The most mystical think the Stone is the spiritual junction of Heaven and Earth—it *is* the Holy of Holies.

"Now ultra-orthodox Jews want the Temple Mount back," Dani said.

I shook my head. *Not without a war between Israel and the entire Muslim world*, I thought. If that happened, we might all get the *Revelations*-prophesied Armageddon some believe would precede the Second Coming of Christ.

Dani nodded in silent agreement.

Farther west, dying sunshine outlined the Church of the Holy Sepulchre, supposedly the site of Jesus' death, burial and resurrection. The basilica has been a source of dispute among Christians for hundreds of years.

In 1853, to keep peace in the holy shrine, the Ottoman Sultan ordered a division of ownership with common areas for the church's seven sects. Known as the Status Quo, the edict said everything must stay the same as it was at the time of the decree. Consequently, as Jerry had pointed out, a ladder sits on a ledge above the church's main entrance—exactly where it's been for over one-hundred-sixty years. But fistfights still break out between the church's feuding Christian brothers and priests, and to this day, a Muslim family keeps the key to the church.

When we'd visited the church earlier in the trip, the men who claimed dominion over the basilica moved in groups performing daily rituals, their brown, black, or white robes marking their separateness from each other and from the crush of Christians who pushed in to touch holy places. In the elevated Calvary room, legions of people genuflected in front of a candle-lit gold altar. On the church floor, prostrate women feverishly rubbed scarves on the Stone of Anointing, supposedly the slab where Jesus' body lay after crucifixion, where his mother would have touched his wounds and washed his body and wrapped it in linen for burial. The women held the scarves to their faces as if there was some absolving grace in the vestiges of sorrow. Under the rotunda, hundreds of pilgrims snaked toward the Aedicule, the venerated site of Jesus' tomb and resurrection. Knowing my husband would never wait in such a line, I'd said, "Let's go." The fresh air and sunshine eased the tension I'd felt in Christianity's holiest place.

Breaking into my reverie, Dani said, "I told you my family is Christian, that we've been here for hundreds, maybe thousands of years, and that I live in a Jewish neighborhood and send my kids to Jewish schools."

He swallowed and looked directly at us, then off to the west where the sky filled with a thin afterglow. "When I tried to take my family to Disneyland, my seventy-year-old mother was strip-searched at Ben Gurion Airport."

"I don't understand," I said, lost in the image of my own mother subjected to such an indignity.

Dani shrugged, a glint of bitterness in his jaw. He nodded toward the shadows creeping across the valley. "If the Messiah came today, he would have to cross a Muslim cemetery, rip away the massive stones that block the Golden Gate, destroy the Dome of the Rock, and restore the Temple on the Temple Mount."

I sighed and pulled my arms close across my breasts, conserving my own heat against the chilling air as dusk drained away the warmth of the sun.

On our last day in Israel, after seeing firsthand the complicated realities of the Holy Land—where Christian clergy fight over the smallest of holy spaces, where an elderly woman can't go to Disneyland without being strip-searched at the airport, where young people, out for a night of fun, are slaughtered by another young person disenfranchised in his ancestral land—a t-shirt slogan became a sad angel whispering in my ear. Its ragged white letters on a black background stopped my final stroll along Tel Aviv's beach promenade. The forty-something who sported it pushed a blonde-haired toddler in a stroller, oblivious to the weight of the message he carried on his chest: "Some Things Can't Be Fixed."

It could have been the name of a rock song I was too old to know, a new mantra expressing the ennui of a generation caught in the middle, a typographic sigh whipped off by an artist looking for a quick buck in wearable one-liners.

I didn't know what it meant to that young man enjoying a

Sabbath afternoon with his sweet-faced daughter, but I knew what it meant to me. That commercialized verbal shrug codified the contradictions of the Holy Land: its promise of peace, the millennia of conflict.

I wanted to ask him, "Do you believe that? Can you, as a father?" But I passed him with a secret sadness because I accepted its resigned truth.

Sixteen of the twenty-one young people who died at the Dolphinarium Discotheque were under the age of twenty; some were only fourteen years old.

Just ask the mothers of those fourteen-year-olds: Some Things Can't Be Fixed.

Donna Love Wallace

Finishing Touch

~ a breast reconstruction poem

A strip mall reclines
among rural, rolling hills. Little Vinnie's
Tattoo parlor, lacks a clinical
vibe—pool table, cue sticks,
leather chairs, animal skin rugs.
African ritual masks fix their gaze
toward the hallway where muted voices
hover behind black-curtained doorways.

In the tattoo room, I thumb through
back issues of *Rolling Stone,* then
strip to the waist, unfold a paper drape.
A room of mirrors where art and artifacts
replicate — a horde of animal bones,
sculpture and scrimshaw. The Twins
blend in despite their plain faces,
thin-lipped scars of smile & smirk.

A dozen ink pots like small communion
cups hold hues of blue, blush, tawny brown.
As he mixes a tinted elixir, my desires dissolve.
I tire of all decisions but this: to trust the artist.
Do you feel anything? Michelangelo inquires.
Nerves severed, I am numb under the tattoo gun—
only tiny bolts of lightning strike
far below the silicone:

                                        the last
            sensation
                        I will feel
                                    so near

Helen Rossiter

The Girl on the Bridge

The moment Jason walks in the door, Liv knows that something is wrong. His text two hours earlier said simply, "Running late", but now he's home and he doesn't smile or kiss her, nor does he look at her as he kicks off his boots and hangs his wet jacket behind the door.

Liv puts a hand on his back. "You're frozen," she says. "Do you want me to heat some soup, or did you eat already?"

Jason walks to the sofa and sits on the arm, watching the flames of the gas fire that barely heats their apartment. "A girl jumped off the Ferris Bridge," he says. "I was helping the cops look for her."

"Oh Jason, that's terrible," Liv says. "What happened?"

He still doesn't look at her as he tells her that he'd been walking home along the river, and when he looked up at the bridge from the place they call The Point, he saw a girl standing on the railings. She was wearing a white shirt, billowy and transparent so that the lights of the cars crossing the bridge illuminated her figure. Liv feels a flicker of surprise that he describes this in such fine detail.

The police arrived within five minutes of his 911 call, Jason continues. They searched with flashlights, but it was too dark under the bridge and they could see nothing. Liv knows the river. She has lived beside it all her life. In winter, it runs slow and heavy as oil, its surface flecked with bands of ice, and there is a patina of tranquility that hides the turmoil beneath. Jason tells her that the police say the current would have carried the girl downstream and that she couldn't have survived. Not in water that cold. For the first time, he looks directly at her. "I would have jumped in myself but it was too dark to see anything."

"I'm glad you didn't," Liv says, and she puts her arms around him, feels the muscles of his arms and the way his heart beats against her breasts. She leads him to the kitchen and pours him a glass of wine. While he drinks, she heats the soup she'd made earlier in the day, then watches as he dunks his bread and chases pearls of barley around the bowl with his spoon.

"Maybe I should go and look for her," Jason says. "Maybe she's still alive."

"The police are there," she says. "Besides, they said she wouldn't have survived."

Jason pushes his bowl aside and finishes the last of his wine. "They could be wrong," he says. "Maybe she's a strong swimmer. Maybe she made it to the bank, further down. I have to go and look for her, Liv." His voice pleads. His eyes beg for her understanding.

"The police will find her," she argues. "And you know no one can survive in that water in these temperatures."

He walks out of the kitchen and she hears the closet door open in their bedroom, and when he comes back into the hallway, he's shrugging his arms into a dry jacket. He wraps a scarf around his neck and searches among the mesh of hats and coats and sweaters that hang behind the door. She finds a hat for him and pulls it over his hair and ears, then reaches for her own coat.

"I'm coming with you," she says.

"No, you stay here. Just in case."

"In case what? In case the police call? Didn't you give them your cell number?"

He stands in front of her, and there is a look in his eyes that worries her. Angry, sad, guilty even. "I don't want you coming with me," he says. "I won't be long."

Once, he'd have asked her to go with him, would have wanted her beside him, but lately there's been a distance between them, something that is new and raw, and instead of arguing, she lets the door close behind him and she hears him take the stairs two at a time. She watches from the window as he runs down the street, a pale, spectral figure under snow that's turning to sleet. He melts around the corner, and his footprints are ovals of sludge under the street lights.

She waits for twenty minutes, then texts him. "Are you all right?

Please come home", but he doesn't reply. She calls his phone but it goes straight to voice mail. And then, just as she's decided to go out and look for him, she hears his footsteps on the stairs.

"I was worried about you," she says, then with a sharpness she can't hold back, she asks, "So did you find her?" although she knows the answer. She helps free him from his jacket and it falls to the floor, wet and shapeless as spilled paint.

"No," he says.

"Come to bed." She takes his hand and he follows without resistance, leaving a trail of damp clothes across the floor. He climbs into bed beside her and she opens herself to sex, but he turns away and is soon asleep. She lies on her back and watches the lights from passing cars play tag across the ceiling. She thinks of the girl who jumped, and of the river murderous with ice, and of the girl's family who will be waiting for her to come home. She wonders how Jason can sleep so easily.

Liv is up early. It's still night outside and the clouds are low and heavy, but there's enough light from the street that she can make out the contours of Jason's face on the pillow, the shadow of new stubble on his chin. Once—was it yesterday? —his face had been soft, boyish, but now she sees a hardness and maturity that's new. Perhaps seeing the girl jump, perhaps witnessing something like that has changed him overnight.

She pads to the kitchen in bare feet and turns on the radio to wait for the local news. If they've found the girl, she'll wake him and let him know. They'll mourn her as they mourn other unknown victims of random accidents with a fleeting grief, and then they'll continue with their lives.

There is nothing on the news but the usual dreck of local politics and factories closing, a multi-vehicle crash on Easy Bend and a warning that the warm front blowing up from the mid-west will turn the sleet to heavy rain later in the day.

Jason doesn't ask if there is news of the girl. His hair is still wet from his shower and he smells warm, of soap and aftershave. He's dressed for work (he is a partner in a small advertising agency) and his tie is knotted loosely around his neck. He tells Liv he will be late home—he has an appointment with a difficult client.

"Will you call the police?" she asks. "About the girl?"

"Of course."

"It's only just daylight." Liv goes to the window. The sleet has already changed to drizzle, and clouds have taken the tops off the office towers across the river so that they look bombed out and broken. "They've probably only just begun to look for her."

He doesn't answer and kisses her goodbye, but his kiss is perfunctory and it brushes the side of her mouth. She wants to let him know that he cannot feel responsible for the girl, but he leaves too fast. He texts her half an hour later to say that he's now in his office and he signs off with two kisses, xx.

All morning, Liv listens for news of the girl, but there is nothing. She's not really surprised. Suicides happen all the time, especially at this time of year, and most go unreported. She wants only to have confirmation that the girl has been found for her family's sake, and for Jason's.

Around noon, she wraps herself in layers of scarves and sweaters and a waterproof poncho, and she walks the ten minutes to a nearby coffee shop. The Ground and Pound serves thirty different types of coffee, and 'home made' pastries and sandwiches are displayed in a case under the counter. The girls behind the counter wear espresso colored uniforms. One of them, a girl with a shaved head and a line of tiny diamonds above her left eye, greets Liv with a small wave and asks, "The usual?"

The girl's name is Jane, which Liv thinks is too ordinary a name for a girl who shaves her head. She should be called Charlie or Sam, one of those androgynous names that are favored by girls like her or girls unsure of their sexuality. Liv finds a table facing the counter and she watches Jane make her coffee. There is a tattoo on Jane's wrist and from a distance, it looks like a Greek pillar. Liv waits for Jane to bring her coffee over and takes another look at the tattoo. It's not a pillar, but a scroll, its edges still red and swollen, freshly inked. The scroll is filled

16 *Helen Rossiter*

with cuneiform shapes, triangles and circles and something that could be an animal or perhaps a man.

"New artwork?" Liv asks.

"It's Sumerian," Jane says. "And no, I don't know what it means. I hope it's something intense and proverbial, but with my luck it's probably about some dickhead cheating on his wife."

Liv laughs, then asks, "Did you hear anything about a girl jumping off the Ferris Bridge last night?"

"No one's said anything," Jane says, then calls out to the other girl. "Melissa, did you hear that someone jumped off the bridge last night?" Melissa shakes her head, no.

"My husband was there," Liv says. "He saw her jump." And she realizes with a sudden, sharp clarity that Jason has never actually said this, had never said, "I saw the girl jump."

"That's sad," Jane says. "Enjoy your coffee."

Liv pulls out her cell phone and calls Jason. He answers quickly, and she asks if he has talked to the police.

"Yes," he says. "The officer I spoke to said they haven't found her."

"Perhaps she didn't jump."

"Perhaps."

There is a silence that hangs heavily between them before Jason says, "I have to go. Talk to you later."

Liv's coffee tastes bitter and she pushes it aside and walks home through the drizzle, and she thinks of Jane's tattoo.

Jason is home later than expected. His meeting was ultra-difficult, he says, but there is flippancy in his voice that contradicts what he is saying. He asks Liv about her day and she doesn't respond. She leans in to him, expecting to smell the river in his hair, the decay of rotted wood and mud that saturates the air above the water in winter. She smells instead the acrid tang of smoke and something else that is faint and warm and sweet. She pulls back and asks, "Did you hear anything from the police?"

"No," Jason answers.

Liv says, "Maybe she climbed back down and went home to watch TV. Maybe she never jumped." She wants to give him a way out, to allow him to disentangle himself if that's what he needs to do.

"You think I'm lying?" he asks.

"There's been nothing on the news about her, that's all," she says, and turns away.

Seconds pass before Jason replies. "Think what you like, Liv." He goes into the kitchen and she hears him rattling cutlery and opening the fridge. She settles under a blanket on the couch. Law and Order is on TV and she watches it without interest. Jason walks past her to the bedroom and is sleeping when she joins him. She lies down beside him but doesn't touch him, doesn't curl her body around his, and eventually she falls asleep too.

Liv is a freelance translator, and for the next two days, she is tour guide and companion to the wife and twin daughters of a visiting Italian dignitary. She takes them to visit the historical parts of the city and the art gallery and in the evening, she attends the Mayor's Dinner where the double stuffed potatoes and Anjou pears with goat cheese taste like cardboard. She thinks of Jason and hopes that he is home. She sends him a brief text, "Miss you." His reply, minutes later, says simply, "Just finished work."

A taxi takes her home when the formalities are over. It's close to midnight and the route crosses the Ferris Bridge. She notices how brightly the bridge is lit, and how high the railings. It would take effort to climb up there, she thinks, and a girl would need a lot of strength in her arms to pull herself up. Below, she can just make out the black water and a pale slurry of ice. She asks the driver if he has heard of a girl jumping from here three nights ago and he answers with a curt "Nope" and then the taxi is over the bridge and four minutes later, it pulls up outside her apartment building.

There are wet footprints up the stairs, melted slush on the stair treads. She follows them into her apartment. Jason's jacket hangs on the hook behind the door and water drips from the sleeves. His boots are carelessly discarded on the floor. Jason is on the couch, the pages of a newspaper scattered around him. Liv breathes in deeply and there is that faint smell again, a mix of smoke and sweetness that hangs in the air like a bubble.

"They haven't found her," Jason says, indicating the paper. Then, before she can respond, he asks, "How was your evening?"

She tells him about the antics of the Italian twins, eleven year olds going on twenty. "I wish I'd been there," he says.

She knows that he is lying.

There is an old chocolate box on the top shelf of their closet. It's a Whitman's sampler made of tin and the pattern on the lid is scratched and the yellow paint has faded. One corner is dented and there are specks of rust on the hinges. Jason has had this box since he was a small boy, and every so often he will add something, or take something out to show a friend.

Liv knows the contents well. There are tickets stubs for rock concerts and World Series games that Jason attended, and a 1985 Playbill for Biloxi Blues autographed by Matthew Broderick. There are newspaper articles, many of them yellow with age. One is from the Maine Examiner of December 27 1968. The headline reads BABY BORN IN STABLE and the article, without hyperbole, recounts Jason's birth in a barn on Christmas Day. There are other articles that don't mention Jason, but are about events he has witnessed, such as the Great Blizzard of 1978 that buried the north east and destroyed the barn in which he was born. Another tells of a small plane that crashed on the roof of a neighbor's house in 1992, where the only casualty was a small dog struck by a piece of flying metal. There is a photograph cut from a newspaper of Jason shaking the hand of Nelson Mandela in 1990 and another of Jason, as part of a relief effort, clearing rubble after an earthquake in the Philippines. The obituaries of Jason's parents are there too, taken from newspapers two years apart, and there is a single photograph of Liv and Jason on their wedding day.

Liv thinks about the old chocolate box as she walks towards the river, and the stories it contains. It's almost six o'clock, the time that Jason says he saw the girl. Liv comes to the Point, a convergence of sidewalks that meet in a small square in the shadow of the bridge. In the summer, the square thrums with people and pigeons, alive with color and sound, but today the square is empty except for a man whose age and face are undefinable in the gloom. He shuffles past her muttering nonsense to himself and disappears, although she can hear his boots scraping across wet concrete.

The river looks hard this evening, and is the color of copper. A chunk of ice the size of a small refrigerator churns on a finger of current beneath the bridge. As Liv watches, the ice breaks free and floats downstream. The headlights of cars crossing the bridge play against the supporting pillars and reflect off the metal of the empty railings. She tries to imagine the girl standing there, her arms raised, her white shirt floating around her in the wind. She wants to believe that this is what Jason saw, but not for the girl or her family or even for Jason. She wants to believe this for herself.

She pulls out her cell phone and calls directory assistance and is connected to the police non-emergency number. A woman answers and identifies herself as Sergeant Banks. Liv asks if the police have found the body of the woman who jumped off the Ferris Bridge. Sergeant Banks says she hasn't heard anything about anyone jumping and she is confused. She wants to know if Liv is reporting an incident. No one jumped, Liv tells her and hangs up.

She walks home in the cold rain and the apartment is dark and empty. She turns on every light and pulls the Whitman's sampler box from the closet. She wants to read again the stories of Jason's life, to comfort herself with the truths of his life, not with a lie that obsesses them both. She isn't sure their marriage can survive that.

Spring finally arrives with clear skies. The river is free of ice and running high, and it carries the flotsam of winter, dead branches and plastic drink bottles and the occasional small animal carcass on its run towards the ocean. Now that the sun is warmer and the tall buildings offer shelter from the wind, office workers return to The

Point with their brown bagged lunches and the pigeons flock in, looking for crumbs and somewhere to breed. Above, the Ferris Bridge carries its load of cars and buses and trucks and when the sun is at the right angle, its railings are reflected in the water below.

Today, a Saturday, Jason has suggested a drive in the country to shake away the last of the winter blues. He seems unnaturally good humored, as if he is trying too hard. They leave the city in sunlight and their route follows the river which is the color of the sky. At a place where the Nabacun makes a sharp turn to the east, Liv asks Jason to stop the car. It's not a place for sightseeing, and the ground here is prone to flooding, but Liv knows it's where the river gives up its dead, those who have lain for weeks under the ice and now bob to the surface like distorted corks. Only last year and within a day of each other, the bodies of a young boy and a homeless man were found among the tangle of roots and branches that clog the river here.

She recalls a picture she has seen in a National Geographic. It is of an ice bridge high on a mountain, so fragile that if a climber steps on it, the bridge could shatter and send the climber and the remains of the bridge into the crevasse below.

"Let's go back," she says quietly. "Let's go home."

Bradford Philen

Suburban White Girl Love Affair
(Or Stubborn Love)

1.

At the Trinity Wellness Center in west Raleigh, Allison John is stretching Mr. McFerlot's hamstring on the therapy table and Mr. McFerlot says, "did you hear about how them Muslim men up in that house were all tootie fruitie?"

Allison recalls the nightly news footage from the day before: a gang of I.C.E. officers surrounded an unsuspecting, suburban home in Fuquay Varina and, after breaching the front door with a battery ram, dragged out five brown men—all frail and bare-chested, clad only in their boxer shorts—and four women, each garbed in a black burka, a tiny sliver of their eyes showing, holding onto four little children.

"Tootie fruitie?" Allison says. "Mr. McFerlot, where in the world did you hear something like that?"

"On the radio. Anything goes these days, don't it, baby doll?" He's the same age as Allison's father and has a similar good ol' boy charm.

Allison gives him a look.

He did have a gruesome injury. A truck driver, he'd fallen asleep at the wheel and ran head-on into signage at an exit ramp. He was lucky he only suffered a broken leg. "Can't you just see it? One of them Jihadists wearing women's undergarments and leggings, prancing around with his AK-47."

She digs her thumb hard in his thigh.

"Don't get sassy on me, missy, haven't I been working hard today?"

"Play nice, Mr. McFerlot."

"Dang, just telling it like it is. Going to hell in a hand

basket—this whole country—if you ask me."

She digs deeper and he reels and *ouch*es even more, then she lets go and says, "all right, you're ready to cool down."

She walks to retrieve the ice packs for the last part of his rehab therapy, and when she returns, he says, "I heard one of them went to Athens."

She thinks for a beat. "Really?"

"What I heard."

"I went to Athens," she says.

"I figured you went to Cary or Athens one. You're a local gal, right?"

She exaggerates her "yes," like *yeeaas*. "Born Raleigh proud."

After Mr. McFerlot's session is over, Allison rushes to the lounge and rustles through the newspaper, but there are no close ups or names, there's just the aerial, helicopter footage, same as the live news, like something out of some Hollywood action flick. She can't help but think about a fling she had in high school with a boy named Raed.

***

Allison and her husband Tommy have three kids: Elizabeth is four; Eric six; and, TJ—Tommy Junior—nine. She never told Tommy about Raed. It wasn't like Tommy had told her about all of the women he'd slept with, she didn't believe that for one minute. Besides, she'd told her "first" story so many times, about how she'd lost her virginity to Grayson Sanford, her high school sweetheart, she'd almost forgotten that, no, Raed was actually her first. How did that happen anyway, she thinks, staring at the brown men in the photo being whisked away in the blacked-out SUVs. She hadn't thought about *that* in years.

When Allison gets home she cooks Hamburger Helper and throws together a salad that no one but her touches. Tommy has poker with "the boys," so she's on duty for the night with the kids. TJ is easy. He'd just as soon leave the dinner table and read. Eric and Elizabeth are a handful, but Allison manages to get them bathed and calm for bed even though every night, without fail, Elizabeth tip-toes into her and Tommy's bedroom to sleep with them at some point.

The next morning, Allison can't believe her eyes. *The News and Observer* front page reads: "Local Muslim Men Arrested, Accused of Plotting Terrorist Attacks." The ring leader was a forty-something former U.S. Marine who fought the Russians in Afghanistan, was shot in battle and won a Purple Heart, returned to the US, converted to Islam, and lived a relatively quiet family life. David Mahoney, also known as "Saifullah," ran a drywall business and looked like an everyday American Joe: sandy-brown hair, evenly-trimmed goatee, brown eyes, slight and assured grin. The rest of the men were all American citizens, but they were brown and their mug shots looked like they'd been pulled from a forgotten cave. There was Omar Abulaye Yaghi, 21; Muhammad Hassan, 22; Anes El Hadj Sherifi, 45; Zakariya Aly, 32; and then, there he was: Raed Habib Aswad, 37.

Allison feels like she might puke. What were the chances? She had lost her virginity to a Jihadist? Is that what he is? What he was? Feeling dizzy, she paces the kitchen. The coffee machine is gurgling. She looks outside. The grass is green, the summer sun rising. It'll be hot like every other summer day. She breathes, turning again to the newspaper. What were the chances? He was much thicker in the face than she remembered. Bearded and head closely shaven now, his once handsome hazel-blue eyes gazed ghost-like at the camera. She can't believe it.

On Mahoney, one neighbor stated: "I saw the family about every day out walking their dog. They waved. We waved. They seemed like nice folks. Not the terrorist type one bit."

Another said: "Their kids played with our kids. It's crazy. You just don't know this day and age who your neighbors really are."

Allison gets stuck on the line: "If convicted, they could all face the death penalty."

She hears Tommy coming down the stairs. She folds and scoots the paper to the end of the kitchen island. "You look rough," she says when Tommy reaches the room. "You win last night?"

He leans on the kitchen island. "I never win."

She pours him coffee. "You were trying to win with me when you came home. Your drunk hands were everywhere."

"Like I said, I never win."

"Not with little Lizzy there in the bed with us. You know that."

It's a long Fourth of July weekend so the kids are still in their rooms. Tommy turns his attention to the newspaper.

"Eggs and bacon all right?" Allison says, turning to busy herself.

"Mm-hmm. Jesus, my head hurts."

"We're still going to the lake house today, right? I texted Crystal we were."

"Says this one went to Athens. Ally, you see this?"

Not looking to Tommy, she says, "No. We only got three eggs, maybe we just get Bojangles on the way out."

"Fine. Ally, paper says he graduated '98. That's your class. Come here and look."

She sighs. "Let me see." She walks to Tommy. "Which one?"

He points. "Raed Habib Aswad. Did you know him?"

She looks closer. "Him? No, don't think so."

"Holy Habiby, he looks like a terrorist."

"You still smell like booze."

"Trump is right. We should build a wall."

"They're citizens, Tommy."

"You know what I mean. It's just all a little scary, isn't it?"

It is, she thinks. You could get shot at the mall or at church or learn that you lost your virginity to a Jihadist.

Allison's short and still fit. She was a soccer star in high school. Tommy, who played college football, is now just burly, wide, and jock-looking. When they embrace, it looks like his body could swallow her whole. He sells real estate and still eats like he works out each day. Allison's been warning him it's only a matter of time before his metabolism slows down.

"How does something like this happen here anyway?" He says.

She moves back into the kitchen, opening the refrigerator again. "I don't know, Tommy. Maybe we just all eat cereal."

"Never thought you'd hear about this here in North Carolina, you know what I mean?"

A few minutes pass and Allison hears the soft pounding of feet along the upstairs floors. Tommy's still reading the paper. She looks at him. "Kids are up."

"Yeah," he says, "I can't wait to get out to the lake."

"Me too," Allison says, but really she's stuck on *how did that happen?*

2.

Twenty-plus years earlier, *that* started one summer at the Hootie & the Blowfish concert. Allison and Grayson had a bad fight and fast breakup. Allison had first-hand evidence that Grayson hooked up with another girl from a different school. A week before the concert at the Cary Towne Center mall, Allison slapped Grayson in the face and then kicked him in the crotch. Grayson grabbed and shoved her to the linoleum floor. Everyone saw it.

"He's an asshole, a cheater, and he's violent," Crystal Whitley, Allison's best friend said. "You can do better than that."

The Varsity Boys' and Girls' Soccer team captains organized the concert outing. All the players went together. On the lawn of the Walnut Creek Amphitheater, Allison sang "Let Her Cry" drunk at the top of her lungs. She thought the last lines of the chorus, "let her be," was some kind of mantra or epiphany, maybe, about love. That night she made-out with Raed there on the lawn. She'd thought Raed was so cute. They had AP Spanish together. He was new to school, had a different accent and name.

"I'm from Persia," Raed had said in class.

Allison had no idea what that meant. "Wow," she said.

After that kiss at Walnut Creek, they spent the next three weeks in Spanish class passing notes back and forth until Raed finally asked her out:

Dinner at Chili's and then a movie?

They held hands for what seemed like the whole night and on the way home Raed parked behind the Kmart on Western Boulevard and they made out, listening to more Hootie.

A few more weeks passed and Allison fell even harder for Raed. Plus, she had heard Grayson was dating some freshman girl now. It dawned on her she was the last in her group of girlfriends to "do the deed," which is how Crystal talked about sex. Allison thought Grayson would have been the one. They'd had so much history, and, well, she'd always thought they'd be together forever. But why couldn't it be me and Raed forever, she thought.

She was almost seventeen. They had done more than just make out, and she figured he was ready for something more than her jerking him off while he fingered her. One Friday morning in Spanish class, she told him to come over that night when she paged him *143.

"Okay," he said.

She didn't tell him what the night would be about. It was supposed to be on her terms, when she told him it was time. That's how it went with sex, Allison was sure. She imagined them lying naked on the couch—or in her bed—hugged up like a pretzel, post-coital. They'd fall asleep together and that would be perfect.

She didn't tell him her parents were out of town either. She paged him at 7:16 pm and waited. When the phone finally rang, she said, "Raed, is that you?"

"Hey."

"You're not on the way yet?"

"Now?"

"Raed! I told you this morning to come over as soon as I page you."

"I just got out of the shower."

She could hear him rustling around his bedroom she'd actually never seen. His parents had rules. *Good Grades* was a rule. *No girls in the house* was a rule. It wasn't that extreme. She had a few crazy Christian friends whose parents had similar rules about grades and the opposite sex. "Hurry," she said, "tell your parents you have a big test to study for or something like that."

"I'll be there soon," he said.

She imagined his room was like Grayson's: messy and gross. Clothes, towels, and dirty, sweaty socks thrown everywhere. Raed was still cute though. So cute.

She got the TV room in the basement all ready. She brought down her favorite pink fleece blanket from her bedroom, the one with the frayed edges that smelled like the kiwi-strawberry Body Shop spray. She popped popcorn and set two cokes on the coffee table. She rewound *Aladdin* in the VCR and played with the lamps so the room was light enough so that Raed could put the condom on the right way, but dim enough so he wouldn't notice the pimple on her forehead she'd tried to cover with the concealer Crystal told her to try.

Back to her bedroom, she gazed at herself in the mirror how she thought models gazed at the camera in those Abercrombie & Fitch advertisements, which was something like a sexy pout. She decided to wear her grey, loungy sweatpants and a blue, long-sleeve t-shirt that read "Athens High Conference Champs 1995-1996." In the back of her top dresser drawer, where she'd stuffed scarfs and gloves, there was a box of three UltraThin LifeStyles condoms that

Crystal gave her. She'd said that the thicker ones always hurt worse. Allison took the box from the drawer, thought for a moment to just take one, but then put all three in her sweatpants pocket.

By the time she got back downstairs to the basement and lit one of the scented Yankee candles her mother kept in the bathroom closet, she heard a soft tapping on the front door. She rushed upstairs. "Hey," she said, opening the screen door for Raed.

He was smiling. "Hey, sorry I'm—"

"No," she said. "It's perfect. Really." She took his hand.

Allison's parents weren't the hovering, overbearing type. As long as she did well in school, which she did, and stayed out of trouble, which she did, she was "left to her own devices and whatnot," which is how her father put it. At work, Allison's father had won a weekend getaway at a *she-she-foo-foo* bed and breakfast out on the Outer Banks. Allison said she had no interest in either of those. "Plus," Allison had said, "soccer practice. Conference tourney in just a month."

"Fine," her father had said. "Just behave."

Allison nodded, *yes, Daddy.*

***

The dimness of the basement was just as Allison had imagined: perfect. She still held Raed's hand. "You want to watch *Aladdin?*" She said.

"*Aladdin?*" He looked around the room. "I mean, yeah, sure."

They sat on the couch. She took a handful of popcorn and pushed one of the cokes closer to him.

"Thanks," he said. "When do your parents get home?"

"They're not here."

"Not here?"

"They're out of town for the weekend."

"Oh."

She took the remote, pushed play, and then slouched even further next to him. "Your eyes are so...striking. You don't see eyes like yours every day."

"Your eyes are really pretty, too," he said.

On the screen, a man riding a camel through the desert was signing "Arabian Nights."

Allison looked at Raed again and pinched his arm. "Hey," she said.

"Hey."

They tongue kissed until Aladdin was running through the market with his monkey Abu and then they stretched out on the couch. Allison lay in front of Raed and handed him a pillow to prop his head so he could see the movie. She took his arm and hugged it in her bosom. They'd never lay like that before.

It was a while before she felt his hand slip to the upper seams of her panties. *Alladin* was her favorite and she knew every line by heart. Just before Jafar turned into the giant cobra, she turned to face Raed. She kissed him once on the lips and started to lick and kiss his neck. She could smell the Polo Sport cologne he'd sprayed too much of.

For some reason, at that moment, she couldn't get Crystal's line "do the deed," out of her mind and thought about even other, way-worse things she'd overheard boys say about sex. She recalled waiting for Grayson one day, back when things were good with him, in the gymnasium lobby, right by the boys' locker rooms, and one boy said something about "when you getting up in them guts, Gray."

She felt Raed's hands get even more erratic and less romantic, so she stopped him. She took her time kissing him on his lips and looking into his eyes. "Hey," she said, pulling the condom wrappers from her sweatpants pocket.

"What's—"

Allison didn't know what to think. Why didn't he finish his sentence? Was he judging her? Would he say no?

"Now?" he finally said.

She kissed him again, thinking, *I wish he was more…*she didn't know what exactly, but she'd made the move that told him yes and like everything else in the world, there's a time to jump in already. At least that's what her daddy always told her.

In the dimness, she got naked and he pulled his boxer shorts to his ankles. She made sure the pink fleece blanket was near and wrapped it over them as he got on top of her. She remembered her girlfriends talk about their first time, like it was something to hurry up and get done. He put on the condom. Crystal said it all gets easier after you do it a few times. It was all awkward and jamming. Allison wished she had something to ease him into her.

"Is it okay now?" He finally said.

"Yes," she said in a whisper.

The deed was done before she knew it. Underneath the pink fleece blanket, she wrapped her arms around him tighter. They both turned their heads to the screen. When the credits started to run, she could feel he'd gone limp.

"It's so hot," he said. "Can we lose the blanket?"

"What's *that*," she said.

"What?"

"What's that oozing?"

He lifted himself up off the couch, like he'd been poked in the ribs. "Shit."

"What?"

"Holy fucking shit."

"What?"
"Shit. Fucking shit."

She looked.

"The condom broke," he said.

She thought, *damn it, Crystal, you and your UltraThin condoms.*

"What if you're pregnant," Raed said, standing, then pacing.

There was no post-coital cuddling. She handed him a box of Kleenex to clean himself.

Allison said, "Relax. Come." She motioned for him to join her on the couch. "Come here. Let's lay again."

"I'm such an idiot."

She watched him look at the broken, goopy condom sitting in a nest of Kleenex on the coffee table. "You're not the only one."

"That's not what I mean." He was still standing.

"What *do you* mean, Raed?"

"You don't get it. My father would kill me. If you're pregnant, my life is—"

"I'm not pregnant. Do you even know what the chances are of that," she said, but she wasn't sure. She'd read recently in *Seventeen* how some girls had gotten pregnant doing a lot less. Something about pre-cum. She'd read too how "copious amounts" of raw and cooked papaya was the natural equivalent to the Morning After pill.

Some time around ten, Allison walked Raed to the door. She paged him throughout the weekend, but when he called back, she noticed he was short. "Raed, what's wrong?"

"Nothing. It's nothing. I have to go."

The next week at school went about the same.

She had to put what she and Raed did somewhere in the universe other than her journal and the calendar hanging on her bedroom wall—she'd drawn a heart around the date—and, well, she had Crystal. Allison told her finally a few days before Homecoming.

"Well, damn," Crystal said, "you sure know how to pick them."

"I thought all guys wanted was sex."

"They do, but you should go on the pill. Keeps your period regular too."

In Spanish class that week, Raed finally passed Allison a note: *did you take the P test?*

I'm not pregnant

U sure?

You're an asshole.

Allison didn't reach for anymore notes from Raed and during halftime at Homecoming, she and Grayson finally started talked again.

3.

Allison and Tommy share a lakeside home at Kerr Lake with Crystal and her husband Danny. The house is big enough for both families and they share everything: the mortgage, lake fees, house repairs, secondary home taxes, and the boats. Crystal and Danny bought a pontoon. Allison and Tommy had an eighteen-foot motor boat.

It's only an hour and a half to Kerr Lake, so by two o'clock, Tommy is steering their motor boat, cruising the summer lake waters, while Allison and the kids are seated and sun-screened, laughing at the heat and the splashing water.

The cell phone reception at the lake is shoddy, so Allison keeps resending her text to Crystal:

Hey girl don't say anything about Raed haven't told Tommy yet

Allison isn't even sure if Crystal knows anything about the terrible Jihadists in Fuquay Varina. They're driving from Atlanta and won't get in until the evening.

When the water clears of jet-skiers and jon boats, Tommy speeds up, ripping through the water. The kids yell giggling *aahs*. Allison wonders if Raed has thought of her. Did he even sign her yearbook? She can't remember. To be fair, she hadn't really thought of him.

There are hardly any waves at Kerr Lake. It's perfect for this type of carefree speeding. "Hang on," Allison says as Tommy cranks the motor boat even faster. She hugs Lizzy in her lap even harder and hears Tommy yell, *yeah buddy!*

***

Over the next few nights, fireworks will be heard across the lake, building more and more until Tuesday, the Fourth, when the professional pyrotechnics will get out in the center of the lake, on a barge or some type of tug boat, and fire mortars, bottle rockets, and 8" shells into the humid sky, while Allison and Tommy and Crystal and Danny and all the kids will watch on the dock or the deck or in the yard. The kids will still be in their bathing suits, eating red, white, and blue cupcakes, and all the adults will be drinking screw drivers out of red party cups, and it will feel like the night will never end, as the summers at Kerr Lake always are and always will be, and there will be Raed eating jail food, whatever that is, praying on his knees on the cold, cement floor, staring at a wall with no life. They'll leave their vacation lake home and return to regular home life. Tommy will go on selling overpriced homes in the Triangle, and at the Trinity Wellness Center, Allison will finally say goodbye to Mr. McFerlot, because he'll be ready to take on his rehab without the help of a physical therapist. What did "plotting a terrorist attack" really mean anyway? That Raed from high school? Allison wouldn't have thought that in a million years. She'll wonder about it all and decide it was just a fling, but Raed will linger back to her mind every once in a while, because none of it feels right, how *those people* are treated and all, but *The N&O* will go back to writing about the $92 million dollar Powerball jackpot and the controversial Bathroom Bill and pre-season ACC football and the Jihadists from Fuquay Varina will become second and third page news and then forgotten for good.

***

Later that afternoon, Allison is in the kitchen starting the Easy-Bake Lasagna and Tommy comes in from outside.

"You're red," she says.

"I fell asleep on the dock."

"Where are the kids?"

"They're fine. Playing and whatnot."

"Come here," she says, "let me put some more sunscreen on you."

He sits at the large dining room table, which is one of those artsy picnic tables designed for inside. The windows are ceiling high and have a view of the back deck and the yard that runs into the lake and the way the mighty pine forests turn and shift the shoreline, it looks like the lake goes on forever.

"You might blister," she says, taking her time to rub the sunscreen on his back.

"I know it."

"You need a beer?"

"Probably need two."

He's a good man, she thinks. Tommy Taylor John. In a way, her life had become all of what she had imagined and hoped for: kids, the neighborhood and house, pool-side summers and cookouts, the State Fair every October. Tommy's a teddy bear and wouldn't hurt a fly. She knows what he'll do even before he does, and isn't that something like love? Yes, Allison thinks, I love my life. It's all certain and safe. And shouldn't it be?

She wonders if maybe that was the whole point of Raed: to remind her to count her blessings. Thank God. Because there had to be a point to Raed the Jihadist. She kisses Tommy on the lips and gets three cold Coors Lights from the refrigerator. She cracks one open for herself. She looks out at the lake. What else in the world can I ask for, she thinks. She takes a sip. What can I do anyway? Call the police about it? Start a book club? The man's a terrorist. It still didn't feel right.

Crystal and her family arrive just before dinner and they bring enough ice cream sandwiches for an army. They talk and laugh and catch up, and after the kids leave the table to catch lightning bugs in the yard, Tommy and Danny pour themselves whiskey and tell their wives they're headed outside to watch the kids.

"Did you get my message," Allison says after the men leave.

"What message?" Crystal moves to the refrigerator to make another vodka-cranberry.

"About Raed."

Crystal gives her a look. "Who?"

"Raed. From high school."

"Who?"

"You know: *Raa-eed*, the cute boy with the hazel-blue eyes."

"Allison, look, to be honest, I barely remember breakfast. The kids, work, one failed marriage, and one that's always hanging on by a thread."

"What happened?"

"Oh, nothing, you know what it's like. Men—"

"Are you and Danny all right?"

"Danny started to shave his pubic hair. He said he wanted to try something new. I said if I caught him cheating, I'd shave off something more than the hair on his balls."

"He's not, is he?"

"I don't think so. You know, it's probably just a phase. What is it, a mid-life crisis?"

"We're not ready for *that* yet, are we?"

"Lord," Crystal says, stirring her new drink. "I don't know. Maybe it's the crisis before the mid-life crisis. Or, maybe he's been watching too much porn on the internet. I don't know. How are you and Tommy?"

"We're fine," Allison says.

They clink their cups.

"Cheers," Crystal says.

"Cheers."

They both drink.

"So, now, who's this you keep talking about from high school?"

Allison hopes her text never goes through. If Crystal doesn't remember, maybe it really doesn't matter. Maybe it never really happened anyway. "It's nothing," she says, and reaches for more vodka. Her cup is half full, mostly cranberry juice. Could it be that simple, she thinks, to forget something or someone like that off the face of the Earth forever.

After she pours more vodka, they join the others outside where the sun has finally faded beyond the lake's horizon. It will be night soon, but now islands of pink and magenta clouds cover the paling sky and the kids *ooh* and *aah* at the lightning bugs. It's all warm outside and there's a hint of breeze. Allison hopes there will be rain at least once over the next few days. She likes to hear water from the sky collapse on the lake.

Later, Allison will tell TJ to stop reading—for the third time—and play with Crystal's boys, who are eleven and eight and sporty and rough. Tommy will keep drinking whiskey and eventually he'll carry Eric to bed. Allison will tuck in Elizabeth. The kids will all be sleeping and the adults will have one more nightcap before bed.

Will there every be an arraignment? Will it ever be clear what really happened at that house? What the "terrorist conspirators" acting as informants for Al Qaeda really did? Will it matter? What about the women and children? But what does Allison have time for anyway? Lizzy wants to take horseback riding lessons and Eric needs to get into another sport because he's got too much energy and TJ, well, Allison wonders if he might be gay, which isn't necessarily a big deal any more is it? Then, there's Crystal's rocky marriage. Those were her priorities, what she was stubborn for.

It was all too much to think about. None of it in the world felt right, but did she have the time or energy to squeeze in anything else? She settles on: what a terrible story it all is.

When Allison and Tommy turn in for the night, they'll get under the covers and then Allison will ask Tommy to pull one of the curtains open just a bit because she wants to see the moon light. Tommy will say he's sore and sunburned, but he'll get up to do it anyway, and then Allison will say, "get the jelly from in the bathroom." She'll watch him move through the slightly moonlit bedroom and when he returns to bed, she'll listen to him squirt the lube and rub himself and say, "are you ready," and Allison will lie on her back and say, "let's do it quick before Lizzy comes in here," and when Allison feels her husband inside her, she'll breathe and relax and hope Crystal makes the Cream Cheese Stuffed French Toast she usually makes on this holiday weekend.

Robyn Campbell

Kintsugi

Some say
the potter
   broke the cup
on purpose
   because he wanted
to see the golden scars.
Well,
I am
Cracked, snapped into
    bits, smashed
into nothingness.
Can I be
Kintsugi?
These scars
beautiful still,
even through those
times when I am
not.
With a soft touch
of sweeping bristles
I
polish imperfections.
Kintsugi
fragile brokenness
loss,
     painful fragments
life's defeat.
Kintsugi
help me pick up
   these

p
        i
            e
                        c
        e
                    s
and glue them back
together again.
With lemon seams,
I will be
Kintsugi.

Jeanne Julian

Smoke Jumper

As a kid you worked that tin top,
frantic for roar and whine
you hammered at it
til your skinny elbow
almost unsocketed,
red yellow blue green
merging as colorless whir,
as a revolving propeller loses
blades, as thought's obliterated
by engine vibrations en route
to the blaze, remembering how
coach said *don't think,*
crouch padded and clad
impervious to any Fahrenheit,
rigged to ride air, unleashing
calm when the radio says
now borne weightless through branches
and thick shifting black billows, squinting,
grappling, in a temple of devastation,
charred spires skewering massed heat and glare
more blinding than the sharpest
glint you ever saw on cleanest
chrome or most ornate gilt altar,
crane your neck you still can't see an out,
work toward the head,
flank the fire, hack back
underbrush and timber,
pump hard enough
it opens like a lotus
   what
tiny spins inside
     dancer
       jumper
         smoke

Trish Sheppard

Suckering

The galvanized bucket waits at row's end.
The ladle props on the side—
inside, water,
tamer of heat.

A look, ever so brief—for black specks—flies, bugs,
she lifts the pitted enamel bowl to her lips.
She side sips, water dribbles down her shirt,
blotches, spreads, merges,
like sweat marks on older field workers.

Too young for wet circles,
she wears her drips with pride— maybe—it looks like sweat.

She turns, faces another row of green leaf-laden stalks.
Eyes scan for small, sprouted leaves— tobacco suckers.
Removal needed, she grasps the base and snaps.

Time to move on.

She bends over—snaps—tosses.

The trampled earth receives.
The sun withers, shrivels the sappers.
Remaining leaves radiate, glisten green.

Legs weary, she stands,
dimness appears, she steadies.
Visions– ruffled, aqua feathers scalloped black,
domed cage, fabric cover.

Parakeet, a parakeet,
she'll buy one
call him, Peety.

She stills a moment, recovers.
The last row, the last plant, she bends.
Snap.

Dollars gather in her mason jar, unfolded, counted,
dream upon dream.

Paloma Capanna

Adopted. Adoptee. ~~Adoptive Parent~~

I am. Both. Adopted and adoptee. It's funny. I didn't used to think of myself that way. All my life, I have known this fact and it was no big deal. I found my birth parents in my 30s and it was super.

It was a normal part of the adoptive family conversation growing up, especially at holiday dinners with extended family. At some point, someone would invariably get into it, and another person would say, "Aren't you glad you aren't going to grow up to be like Uncle _____ or Aunt _____? You're lucky to be adopted." We loved this uniqueness. We could blame all my faults on the parents we didn't know and we could claim all the credit on the hard work being invested by my adoptive parents. "Mother" and "Father" and "Grandmother" and "Grandfather" and "Cousin" and "Aunt" and "Uncle." It was all family and that was how it was supposed to be.

At some point in my legal career, I learned about the adoption process. Marveled at the extent of it. Heard about foster care. Considered what did it mean that there was a sixweek lag between my date of birth and the date we celebrated every year as adoption day, the date my parents picked me up. It was odd not to know the hospital I was born at, but not uncomfortable. And I was used to saying, "I don't know" to every doctor who asked for family medical information.

But then this thing happened. This minute of awareness. And then, another one.

I had failed to appreciate the prejudice against children who are adopted and the birth parents who give them up. We are viewed as rejects. As ones unloved by our birth mothers. As having some kind of an inherent defect. Of being unworthy of the special kind of love a biological parent gives only to a biological child.

It happened shortly after I got married. In England. In a British country manor house that an American would refer to as a "castle," except that I was raised by an adoptive British father, and so I knew better. It was an idyllic fairytale setting, by any cultural standards.

In the days after the wedding ceremony, at a country farm in the Yorkshire region, this woman and her husband and their two young daughters had us over and cooked us dinner and we stood there talking as the girls and Sam (age four) ran about, in and out of the house, in towards the adults, out towards the trampoline. Sam is my step-son, who I don't think of as a "step." There is no "step" that distances him from my heart and I cannot imagine loving any child more…but that's a whole separate kind of "identity" question, isn't it?

So, picture this gorgeous farm kitchen. Big and sprawling and with a table to seat every useful farm hand, all leading out to picture-perfect gardens, framed by old metal greenhouse material that provided a door to the outside and, at the same time, brought the outside in.

She-who-shall-remain-nameless-but-knows-who-she-is pulled something hot out of the stove, perhaps a chicken, in a blackened metal pan. She bent over to pull it out, then put it up on top of the stove, insufficient protection for her hands through the tea towels resulting in a clatter as she let go of the pan too early. Between us there is a counter. There's grazing stuff upon that counter, like smelly English cheeses and Carr's Table Water Crackers and grapes and other healthy bits. We chatted. We were two women in a kitchen who finally had a moment because the men went off to look at tractors and black-faced sheep and other important, manly business and the children had blessedly absorbed themselves outside on the trampoline. Late on a sunny day in July. A healthy dinner about to be served in the long, late angles of a blessedly sunny day in northeastern England.

I said something out of turn about having children or possibly adopting – *or maybe she asked?* – I don't clearly recall. I was in my mid-30s and my new husband and I had already been together for a couple, two or three years, before getting married.

Then, there it was: her mouth, moving, as she looked at me and said, "You can say all you want but you won't love them as much as if you have your own."

Slap!

Wow.

She proceeded to pontificate the point at me. My facial expression a sufficient response for her to feel that she could and should continue to educate me on the probable mistake we would be making if we were to *adopt.*

Blood pounded in my ears. *What did this say about what she thought about my relationship with Sam? Didn't I adopt him as surely as I married his father? There is the biological, there is the legal, and there is the truth of one's heart. What is she saying?*

It was all very British. The way they manage to do it. That look down their noses. That tone in their voices. If you believe in divine right monarchy, I suppose even the little people consider themselves entitled to hold opinions designed to denigrate others. *God help me I hate how I can do the same damn thing right back when I'm pushed and shoved and diced into little toothpick-ready cubes!*

Twenty years ago, when this happened, I had nowhere near the confidence to handle such prejudice and condemnation. It was also a first and I'd no thought on how to handle such a thing.

Instead, I said, "You do know that I'm adopted?"

I honestly can't remember what happened next. I suppose the children came running back in, all sweaty and red-cheeked and excited and talking all at once and the men re-entered with tales that required an audience. "Dinner's ready! Go wash your hands!" and other commands Anna will have been shouting to get everyone properly into their places to *ooh!* and *aah!* over her cooking and no, she didn't need any help, thank you!

No, what I do remember was the sting resulting in dissociation that left me distanced from everyone else for the rest of the otherwise lovely evening. I remember the scene at the front door as we made promises to see them later in the week and before we left to go home to the States, the kisses, and the "Ta-Ra!" and the driving the rental Merc away across the farmhouse-gravel courtyard of the gentry, before pulling out onto the wrong side of the roadways (meaning right), passing under yellow highway light after yellow highway light, as Sam and his father fell soundly asleep for the hour's drive in Britain with an

American behind the wheel.

Three years later, again it happened, in Sodus Bay, New York, on a different, hot, summer day, surrounded this time by hordes of shrieking children, loving the water and the inflatables and red hots coming off the grill. Who knew where to find so-and-so? There were enough kids that they were watching out for each other and there were enough adults acting like children that either him or him or him was the more likely to need a trip to the Urgent Care.

This time it was a stranger. A woman. A mother. A mother of an infant. Part of a circle of women, passing around the baby, chirping up a storm.

Snap!

Words like "can't expect" and "love" and "someone else's kid" and "those kinds of women shouldn't call themselves mothers."

The one woman I knew who I thought was a friend just looked at me. Linda knew I was adopted; she knew I was offering adoption as an option to the guy-next-door to whom I was married. Linda's eyes opened slightly, not out of discomfort with the comment, but worried I might create a social faux pas. She broke in with "well, you know the price of tea in China is starting to go up" or some other equally disjointed grouping of words.

For a second time, I said, "I'm adopted."

And, for a second time, it triggered nothing more than a relentless tirade of opinion, this time from the new mother who felt herself empowered and entitled to cast judgment on every woman who ever had a child and given that child to adoption for whatever the reason. There was no sympathy. There was no empathy. There was no opening of her arms for "those children," even as she allowed me, a total stranger, to hold her child. I handed this precious girl off to my then husband, who made the fatal male mistake at precisely that moment of walking over to a circle of women passing a baby. I walked away. And I never went back to that cottage or those people and I found excuse after excuse to not put myself in such a situation, again.

The trees in that back yard at the side of the bay seemed far too tall and close and shady. I see the leaves as I sit here now, upon the floor, leaning my paper and pen upon my coffee table containing a Navajo sand painting of the spiritual beings known as "Yei."

But I can neither work quietly on this essay, nor can I break away from it. I grab up all the pages and the pen and go to the nearest public library to keep writing down all these words. A public space. A comfort zone. I surround myself by books and literate people and pretend there isn't anyone here who'd treat me badly or let me suffer.

I stake out a chair with some amount of deference to H.R.H., the Queen of England. The blue, swirly patterned fabric absorbs my fingers as I place them, arrhythmically left, right, upon the arms. Sit erect. Refuse to lean into the back. Become the cliché du jour: keep calm and carry on.

I also wish to thank the Academy for allowing me to lie as I carry around my pain. Move it around from place to place. Update the style of the suitcase to be contemporary to the scene. It's the luggage tag that insists on saying "JANE DOE" in neat, block print, as if I'd ever lose it? As if a baggage man would be fool enough to steal it?

Pretty please!

Do me a favor!

Please steal this bag!

Imagine the laughter if this bag should actually whiz on by. The big man in the pinny, shouting, "Vinny! Check this one out! Some kinda crazy going by!"

Up above – *there!* – the wiry climber, the guy sent up when a bag gets stuck. He motions back with two open arms, mouthing, "What?" He's wearing industrial ear covers. His coworker points at a particular bag. Vinny looks around. It's on its way. It's rising up to him.

It temps our Vinny. It truly does. Wouldn't that be a defense if he walked it out the door tonight? His boss would laugh out loud. The armed guard would wind him up. His wife, Regina, might even scold, "Vinny! You can't think the woman was really serious when she put these stickers on her bag?"

Imagine them both, overwhelmed by curiosity, making room on a tired dining room table, dressed up in a Goodwill tablecloth. *Thud!* It lands hard on the surface. Zip. Pull open. Empty. Empty?! But this must be near 30 pounds of dead weight! "Go get a knife. It must be sewn into the seams," they say to each other, then pause, "Jinx!" calls Vinny, first, and Regina gives him a kiss, as they laugh at the joke that must have been played on Vinny by the guys at work.

Truth is, they can't see what's in my suitcase any more than you can, if you sit down next to me – right now – on that empty bench three feet away – right there – in this library, right over there in front of me.

I look too calm. Blue shirt, blue shorts, blue stripe upon my socks and this blue pen. I match the chair. I look too smart to be stupid. I am too highly educated to be naive. A professional, even in activewear. Someone stops to ask me the time because I look like someone who would know.

No, this weight's invisible until I give it words. Until I write it down, it plays hide-and-seek. It's out of view, even from me.

And so, here's what comes next. A sequence of memories that skips across time and gets all out of order. It's not an easy business, this business of contemplating my "identity" and all that's bundled up after some fifty years of living and breathing and walking about the planet.

He (the then husband) eventually admits, "I don't know if I can adopt a child," and the floor slides out from under my feet. This came after – several months after – the lawyer, the retainer, and the beginning steps towards adoption. The brochures, the on-line, the networking, the agency selection, the home study starter questionnaire. The calculation of costs involved; the tax credit discussed with the accountant. The pros and the cons of a girl versus a boy. How commercial aircraft are designed three seats to an aisle and how now we'll be split into two rows. We even looked at single engine aircraft for six persons, instead of the four person models we had been shopping shortly before we shifted from conversation to execution of the adoption project.

It came after I thought to myself about every woman carrying a child that might become our child. The prayers I prayed in those months, imagining her, imagining you, my daughter, my son, my younger sibling to Sam. How I thought about fresh food and walks through the woods as you went through your own process, while I went through mine.

I was healthy. There was no reason I couldn't have children. But, it turned out he couldn't any longer, and so – whatever – Sam was the son of my heart and his friend Beth was my daughter given by the universe, and so let's just grab another and share this love, this life, this house, these schools, these travels, these adventures, the story books Sam was rapidly outgrowing, the pjs from his British grandmother that were way too short and not fire resistant. The bottles haven't been on the top shelf of that kitchen cupboard for all that long, so set up the crib and move things around and voilà – it can be a baby-ready nursery.

The kids were aware – Sam and Beth, his equally little friend. We were all three of us drawing together one afternoon when the two of them started asking questions like "Can I name her?" and "How old will she be?" and "Will she speak English?" The three of us could simply have hopped in the truck right then and there and picked her up and it would have been just that seamless.

There was even a nursery set up. For a few hours, anyway. He set it up. God knows why. I returned from a trip abroad, and he left my suitcase in the kitchen, and he brought me straight into that room, and there was this fully set up nursery down to a little yellow blanket that he'd gone out and bought that said "You are my sunshine" and an outfit that he'd gone out and bought that said "Little Sister." And then he handed me a full-sized white envelope. And then he closed the door on me in that nursery where he wanted me to sit by myself in the rocking chair and read his multi-page, typed out letter that started, "I don't know if..."

It was light when I got home.

It was dark when he knocked and came back into the room.

I never did read that letter. I told him I'd read it when I hadn't. Couldn't. Knew right then and there any hope of adoption was gone. That being adopted wasn't going to be good enough for him. Wasn't going to result in his loving *that* child any more than -- Any more than what? Than a parent who didn't love their child enough to fight to keep the child. Wouldn't allow him to treat another child as equally as he treated Sam.

He took down the nursery that very night. Had set it up by himself. Took it apart by himself. My parents were arriving for a visit the next day and he wanted the guest room restored. My parents arrived, and they and their suitcases inhabited that room for the next, several days.

He occasionally looked at me when he thought no one was watching. He announced he had to leave for a business trip that had suddenly come up. He walked out and left me there with my parents asking me where he went. Eventually, they went away, too.

The house fell silent then. Sam was with his mom. His dad was off on a business trip. And I sat down on the same sofa where I had been looking out the window at our big, beautiful backyard full of willow trees and towering pines that swept out to Lake Ontario and I couldn't even cry. I simply stared. Until I slept.

The next year, I held a massive garage sale and I sold that crib to grandparents who were thrilled to have an all wood crib for their visiting grandchild. Their daughter had just had her first baby. I brought it down out of the attic to the garage for the sale. It fit in the back of their SUV, even with the child's car seat set up behind the driver's seat, and off it went.

Somehow, as it all started falling apart, I never did get around to telling the husband that at the meeting with the adoption lawyer he missed right before my trip, Greg had said with no small amount of glee, "What do you mean you're part Indian? That's great. That accelerates the whole thing. Are you willing to take in an Indian? If so, this whole thing can happen right away."

I was adopted as an infant. I am an adoptee. I am not an adoptive parent.

Michael Gaspeny

World on a String

I talked to Sinatra when I was ten.
Uncle Luigi held the phone. Frank joked,
"Keep those high hopes, Kid, and your uncle
off the sauce!" *High Hopes*, I knew Frank's hit by heart.
Luigi raised an amber glass, crossed his eyes. I laughed.
Because I was chubby, he dubbed me "Biscuit Pants."
His call jolted my spine like a buzzer.

Arrayed in blaring colors, hailed at every corner,
Luigi had brio and inside angles on sporting events.
Every bettor in Bayonne wanted a word
with the swami of Madison Square Garden.
I lugged the rewards of being Luigi.
You could barely see me, behind fruit baskets,
wearing bobbing salamis. Once, we played
catch with a peach he let me eat.

Now when I shake the cigar box from Luigi days,
the pit rattles among swizzle-sticks and bits
of a bat-whacked yo-yo, once glossy black,
sparkling with glass diamonds—a gift
from the street to Luigi to me.

"Watch out, Biscuit Pants!" he warned,
flicking cat's cradle in my face.
"Walk the dog!" he announced,
spinning the yo-yo down the hall.
"Hold it till you get to the grass!"
he teased, squeezing my nape.

That winter, love taps
from my Louisville Slugger.

Bonnie Larson Staiger

Pendulum of Ordinary Time

The cock's crow heralds first light

on a mother nursing her newborn

and down the road – it wakes

a grandfather's wizened fingers.

Time tenders pot-roast

and potatoes under a cast-iron lid

infusing Sunday afternoons

with onions and newsprint.

It overhears geese honking

overhead as they wing southward

through the night – migrations

of a thousand years.

Time sands over moments

and decades soften like waves

vanish into shoreline – passing

at the speed of Wednesday.

Courtney Lynn Camden

The Unimaginable

When I was younger, hardly in high school, I used to blurt it out. As if there was nothing else to say that could be more important.

There wasn't, not really.

But the subject of death is not taken lightly when brought to attention by a fifteen year-old outcast. I'd tried confiding in a theater teacher at one point, telling her about the memories I dreamt of too often, seeking commissary. She instead rang the alarms of the guidance counselor, whose *patience and comfort* I did not need nor desire.

There are things we can do to make you have friends! We can change you!

She'd said this from the cushy, swiveling chair. I looked up from the floor and laughed quietly in her face.

That's nice, but I don't want to be friends with these people. They're unkind.

She frowned back at me, clicking her tongue, and eventually my mother had to come in and ask her to stop calling me away from class for *emergency therapy sessions.*

My friend was an actress as much as I was, but also very popular. Not in the kind of way where you think, *they're totally going to peak in high school and then end up working at Trader Joe's.* Laila was incredibly genuine and frustratingly kind. There was a point when she undoubtedly grew tired of my clinginess, however, she continued to ask how I was in the hallways, remembered my birthday, and hugged me after I told her I'd been accepted to a regional theatre program.

As time went on and I became less humiliating to be around, we grew a bit closer again. The height of our resurged friendship, whether it was one of real value or well disguised pity I will never know, was during the winter production of *James and the Giant Peach*.

"Hey, Laila?" I said, already dreading the fact that I was unable to reel my voice back in and effectively un-ring the bell. I had just thirty minutes before the director would call us.

"Yeah?" she said, not yet looking away from the mirror where she was applied sleek catlike eyeliner that I wouldn't master for another six years.

"We're, uh, we're still friends, right?" I wasn't savvy enough to recognize the desperation in my sentence structure, but Laila seemed to take it in stride. She turned to face me, smiling bright.

"Yeah, of course! We're cool." She said, and my shoulders sagged in clear relief. We finished putting on our makeup before taking our places backstage, irretrievable.

Two weeks later, the entirety of my elitist private school came together in the relatively new auditorium for our first assembly since spring break. I walked past rows of students before eventually claiming a seat in the far left corner. For the first time in years, their eyes were not focused on me in mocking detachment, but zeroed in on the front of the room where images of Laila were splayed across the projection screen. I watched as she appeared skating through a routine at the local ice rink. The photograph disappeared and was replaced with one of her on the beach, caught mid-turn towards the camera, sunglasses on and hair flowing.

There was a blur of speeches from the headmaster and dean of students, both men that I openly opposed in the same vein that Kate McKinnon opposes Donald Trump. They spoke of Laila's academic achievements, her participation in the arts and success in sports before announcing a scholarship in her name. They spoke with quiet sincerity and it was the only time in my life that I did not hate them with everything in my marrow.

Soon after, students and teachers were invited up to the podium to share their memories of Laila. Instead of the mob I had expected, there was not a soul but the science teacher, who spoke of how Laila always brought in cupcakes for Earth Day, and a single sixth grader, who began to cry the minute she was handed the microphone.

The headmaster had risen from his place in the crowd in preparation to end the whole affair when I finally forced myself to stand. When I reached the podium I told myself that this was just another monologue, an audition in which I might shed a tear for dramatic effect and nothing more. I cleared my throat.

"Well, uhm. Laila and I were in a few shows together. *The Wizard of Oz*, and *The Music Man*, and *James and the Giant Peach*. She was a wonderful singer, and such a great actress." I paused, and looked down at the girls who knew her best weeping in the front row.

"She was such a good friend. You could never be upset with her, no matter what. She was *everyone's* friend. And I don't know how we're going to get through this. But, we're a community, so . . .So, we will." I told this lie about my school, true tears in my eyes while gritting my teeth.

I stepped down from the podium with shaking legs, the headmaster offered me his hand and I took it without thinking. The bell rang, and students scrambled out of their seats. I stood up numbly before vaguely noticing my name being called above the crowd.

I turned, and there was her mother. A wisp of a thing, with three sons by her side.

Thank you, thank you, thank you.

She called desperately as students pushed in front of me until I could no longer see her.

I didn't go to lunch. I walked past the Science Wing and

through the Languages Hall. I didn't stop until I came to the edge of campus, to the benches where students would beg to hold class once the weather shifted. I stared past the iron fences and out towards the highway. The wind whipped across my face as I waited for the cars to crash into one another.

David Dixon

Death Certificate

I suppose I was wrong on some.
After all, there were more than a few
brought to me for people I never knew.
Hurried flipping through pages of tattered
charts now marked "expired" for the
guy from the funeral home is waiting.

Don't write cardiac or respiratory arrest
we were taught nor was I allowed to put
"killed by grief" even when true.

Sometimes EMS calls in the night
and asks "can we move the body"
and I always say "of course" and
"thank you" for these are strange
powers to possess and wield.

I am bemused by the thought that
certificates expire and need renewal
while people expire and need certificates.
This, I think, is a good one liner for
the intern on ICU at 3 am. You may use
it. Perhaps a nurse will smile kindly

and let you sleep an extra 5 minutes
before waking you up to do it all over
again. It can only be funny once.

And so I summon my better penmanship
and attest to no level of mastery
but sign simply
that a work here is done.

Emily Wilmer

Katydid

for Doctors Without Borders

Home a week, sand and dust
still cling to my girl's clothes, fall
out of her boots. Memories lurk
in the shadows. Slow shuffle

of feet, thousands of feet march
through her dreams. Hands strain
for rice, clean water, a place to rest,
a gate to enter.

Babies strapped to mothers' backs.
Toddlers, hushed with hunger,
search for a hand to hold
with gauze wrapped handless arms.

She wonders *How did I stay so long?*

She loves mountain nights
thick with moisture, rise and fall

of katydids droning their lullabies.
Ka-ty-did, she-didn't, Ka-ty-did, she-didn't

Now in our field of sweet
meadow grass a single katydid

lands on her leg, then her hand.
She watches his long leaf-like body,

slender antennae search her palm.
She stretches out onto the warm earth,

waits, listens for the pulsing thrum
that washes a body clean.

Pamela Akins

Hard Candy

Ellie jumped off the back of her father's wagon. Her head throbbed and her hands were scratched from picking cotton. She'd stooped over cotton plants all day, dragging a canvas sack, pulling the bolls with their spiky black casements and white fiber heads. A sharecropper's daughter, she was glad tomorrow was Sunday.

"Eleanor, go help your ma with supper. Just wash up first. I don't want her thinking I work you too hard," Daddy said, while unhitching the mule from the wagon.

Ellie stood on the bottom porch step and beat her dirty overalls front and back. With no breeze to blow it away, the fine black loam swirled around her like a dark veil. When no more soil came off her clothes, she climbed the porch steps to the washbasin and washed her arms and hands. She usually wore old cloth gloves in the field, but she hadn't been able to find them this morning. Daddy didn't abide being late, so she'd climbed aboard the wagon with her brothers, Johnnie and Robbie, knowing there would be a price to pay for losing her gloves. The harsh lye soap stung the boll spur cuts on her hands. But Ellie wouldn't complain. "Life is hard, and whinin' don't make it better," Mama often said.

Ellie heard a car rattle into the yard and stop. The front door screen creaked and soft indistinguishable voices followed. Probably Everett, Ellie thought, making a face. He was just too creepy—even if he was Aunt Lucy's beau. She avoided him when she could.

Ellie tossed the dirty water off the porch onto three chickens pecking in the dirt. They squawked and flew out of the way. She poured fresh water and washed her face and neck, her underarms and around inside her shirt. She felt her flat chest—Mama said changes would be coming soon, but not much had happened yet. Ellie didn't mind—she liked the way she was.

Coming into the kitchen, Ellie yelled, "Mama, can I have some tea?"

She wanted a tall glass of the sweet sun tea Mama made in

the summer. She'd been drinking out of a tin bucket all day, and she wanted to get the field taste out of her mouth.

"Not now," Mama called from the parlor, "we're savin' that for supper. And stop that yellin'!"

Ellie glanced through the screen door at the rain barrel on the porch. The rainwater wouldn't be sweet like the tea, but it would be cool and clean.

"Come on in here, Ellie. We've got a visitor."

Ellie made a face again—she didn't want to see that man. Besides, she could almost taste the rainwater.

"Come on, girl," her mother said. "We don't got all day."

Ellie sighed. She patted her curly dark hair, straightened her overalls, and walked into the living room. She did what her mama said.

Mama sat on the blue stiff-backed couch with Lucy, Mama's baby sister. Both were fanning themselves against the heat of the room. Through an open window, Ellie spotted a Model A sitting in the front yard.

"Ellie, you remember Everett McBride?" Of course Ellie remembered Everett—he'd been courting Lucy for six months.

Everett sat across from the two women, his black hair slicked back, his face clean-shaven. A tiny dab of styptic on his sloping chin stood out like a white freckle. He wore a starched white shirt open at the collar, revealing his sunburned neck and its knotty Adam's apple. Sharp creases in his black pants folded over his knees.

"Hi, Everett," Ellie murmured.

"Why, look at that girl!" Lucy said, fanning her skirt out around her knees. She wore a white dress that was covered with little pink roses. Darts in the dress bodice emphasized Lucy's plump breasts. Her light brown hair was piled on top of her head in soft curls. Her grey-green eyes jumped nervously above her rosy cheeks.

Ellie cowered in the doorway, feeling dirty and embarrassed

at the overalls Daddy let her wear when she worked in the fields. She was intimidated by Lucy's beauty. Even Mama had taken off her apron and re-pinned those strands of mousy brown hair that always trailed her at the end of the day.

Mama patted the couch between herself and Lucy. "Come on over here and sit with us like a lady." Ellie did what her mama said.

Lucy gathered her skirt close to her thighs and leaned toward the arm of the couch. Ellie slid in between them, taking care not to brush against her aunt's dress.

Next to Lucy, Mama seemed tired and worn out. Ellie remembered when Lucy came to live with them after Meemaw got sick. No one, not even Mama, would talk about Meemaw's illness. When the church ladies visited, they would roll their eyes toward the bedroom and talk in whispers. But Mama pretended she didn't hear the soft moans of the dying old woman and offered her best homemade cookies in a cheerful voice. Still, Ellie remembered her mother's sad eyes every time she came out of that darkened room.

Lucy had been twelve back then—Ellie's age now. After Meemaw's death, Lucy's sadness lingered a long time. Ellie had thought it would be fun to have an older "sister," but Lucy avoided her and her make-believe games. Besides, Mama and Daddy never made her work as hard as Ellie. While Ellie did farm chores like feeding the chickens or slopping the hogs, Lucy only worked in the house, cleaning, cooking and sewing. But Ellie didn't complain. Lucy was the orphan, the one who needed someone to take care of her. "She only has us now," Mama said.

"Everett, Lucy tells me that you're thinkin' about being a minister. I thought you were doin' pretty well for yourself at the gin," Mama said.

"Well, ma'am, the gin does pay pretty good this time of year, but I feel the Lord a-callin' me." When Everett said "the Lord," he craned his neck up and frowned, like a preacher giving a Sunday School lesson.

Mama touched the Bible on the lamp table next to the couch. "Well, God calls us to many things." Everett nodded as if he knew the weight of God's will.

"So what time will the two of you be back tonight?"

Lucy's cheeks flushed with even more color. She adjusted her skirt and squirmed deeper into the corner of the couch. "I guess ten or eleven. Right, Everett?"

"Yes, ma'am, the church social should be over by then."

"I'll go get a sweater." Lucy jumped up like a fawn leaping out of a bed of leaves. The dress skirt and its pink flowers fluttered about her.

Mama rose, too. "Why don't you take my Sunday wrap? Let's see where it is. Ellie, you stay here and entertain Mr. McBride."

Ellie squirmed on the hard couch. Her arms ached from the day's work and a bug bite on the back of her neck itched. She crossed her hands in her lap, being careful not to rub the scratches on her palms.

"Want a candy?" Everett leaned forward from the edge of his chair, holding a butterscotch between his fingers. Ellie stretched out her hand and opened her palm, ashamed to show the penalties of her forgetfulness.

Everett laid the round candy in her palm and ran his hand along the back of hers. His long fingers were cool against her warm skin. His lips curled open on one side. His eyes held hers.

"You like hard candy?" His thumb traced up her arm.

Ellie nodded, unable to speak.

His hand moved under her overall straps and brushed her right breast. The muscles in her chest tightened. She held her breath.

"You can have more if you like." Through her shirt, his fingers brushed her nipple.

Like a spring stretched beyond its breaking point, her arm snapped back toward her body, knocking him away and popping the butterscotch in her mouth.

Pamela Akins **65**

Ellie leaned back against the couch, pulled herself into a tight core, and looked down at her hands. The room seemed hotter than when she'd first walked in; she could hear the blood pounding in her ears. The candy stuck to her tongue. She was ashamed—she'd put it in her mouth so quickly.

Mama and Lucy appeared at the hall doorway. "Here she is," Mama said as if presenting her most precious belonging.

Lucy looked lovely. Mama's antique silver locket lay in the hollow of her neck and a white cashmere shawl was draped over her arm.

The scent of Mama's cedar chest blended with the burnt butter-sugar in Ellie's mouth. She felt nauseous. She wanted to take a deep breath through her mouth to relieve the tension in her stomach, but she was afraid she'd suck the candy into her windpipe.

"You may be excused, Ellie," Mama said, looking at Lucy.

Everett laid the shawl about Lucy's shoulders. "Don't you look lovely?" He offered Lucy his arm, and she smiled shyly, the color in her cheeks deepening.

"Go on now, Ellie, go to the kitchen," Mama said, watching the couple walk out the front door.

Holding her mouth shut, Ellie walked through the kitchen to the back porch. She dipped the ladle into the rain barrel and took a long drink, letting the cool water flow around the hard candy. When it finally loosened from her tongue, she crunched it between her teeth and washed the butterscotch bits down with another ladleful. The rough pieces scratched her throat as they went down. Ellie thought of Everett's fingertips on her nipple and shuttered.

"Come help me with dinner," Mama called from inside. Ellie took another deep drink before going into the kitchen.

After supper, Ellie helped Mama with the dishes while Daddy filled the washtub with water heated on the stove. Despite being the last to step into the gray and soapy water, she was happy to wash off the day's filth and pull on clean panties and a cotton nightgown. Mama told everyone to go on to bed and said she'd wait up for Lucy.

Baby Bess was already asleep in the crib tucked into a corner of the room Ellie and Lucy shared. The bedroom was hotter than the living room, even though the two windows were wide open. Tiny breezes pushed lightly against the window sheers, but did little to cool the room.

Ellie lay on top of the bed sheet and pulled her nightgown up to her thighs. She could feel the fatigue in her bones. Her back, arms and hands still ached from the daylong cotton picking. She wondered why Everett had given her the butterscotch, why he had touched her that way. Despite the heat, she shivered.

A loud thunderclap broke the night's silence and the sheers on the windows lifted inward with a cooling breeze. Ellie could hear low tones from the front of the house. After a little while, Lucy came into the room, humming "Wildwood Flower." Ellie turned onto her side—she knew Lucy wanted to talk about her evening.

"Hi, sleepy head."

"Hi," Ellie whispered, careful not to wake Bess. "Have a good time?"

"Oh, yes, I had the most *wonderful* evening." Lucy lifted her skirt on each side and sashayed about the room.

While Lucy dressed for bed, she talked about the evening: who was at the social, what the refreshments were, how the grange hall was decorated. To Ellie, it seemed every other word was "Everett," and at every mention of his name, she tasted butterscotch. Underneath Lucy's chatter, Ellie heard the soft alto of her mother's voice and a low baritone.

"Everett's still here?"

"Yes." Lucy pulled a light shift over her head and sat on the edge of her bed. "Your mama's asked him to sleep over. Somethin's wrong with the car, and with the storm comin' and all, she thought it might be safer for him to stay."

Lucy lay down facing Ellie. "He's going to sleep on the couch."

"But tomorrow's Sunday."

"Yes, he'll go to church with us." Lucy lay back on her bed and stretched her arms out under her head. "He'll be here all night," she said dreamily.

After a while, the voices in the living room died down, and Ellie heard Mama's footsteps going down the hall. Lucy tossed and turned, hummed and sighed. The storm passed over with thunder rumbling from one side of the house to the other, and the front behind it cooled the air. Eventually, Lucy quieted and Ellie drifted off to sleep.

Ellie woke slowly. She could feel someone touching her upper thigh. She lay very still, wondering if it was a strange dream. A hand ran along the edge of her panty leg, pushing underneath the cotton band. She opened her eyes slightly to see who was touching her. Everett sat on the edge of her bed, his hand on her thigh, moving toward her private place.

Ellie lay very still, trying to think what she should do. Pretending to be asleep, she rolled over onto her side and Everett's hand slipped out from underneath her panties. He rose and backed out of the room. Once she knew he was gone, she pulled her nightgown down as far as it would go and lay very still, thinking about the touch of his fingers between her legs. She looked over at Lucy who lay with her mouth open, sleeping soundly.

Ellie crawled under the sheet, pulled it up over her head and held it down tight. She felt sick, but didn't want to get up. Scorched sweetness filled her mouth.

Eventually, Ellie heard birds singing in the pecan tree outside the bedroom window. When the rooster crowed, she knew Daddy and Mama would be up soon. Then everyone would get ready for Sunday School.

Ellie didn't know what she should do. She could pretend to

be sick, but Mama and Daddy didn't countenance sickly children. You had to be throwing up or have a high fever to stay home from church. Besides, she would have to look at Everett some time. He was Lucy's beau and he wasn't going away.

Ellie got up quietly and poured water into the basin to wash her face. After dressing in a clean pinafore, she went into the kitchen to help Mama with breakfast, tiptoeing past Everett in the living room, her stomach tightening. He lay sprawled on the couch, his chest bare, his black pants unbuttoned at the top.

While Mama made buttermilk biscuits, Ellie lit the stove, made coffee, and set the dining room table. Daddy came in pulling up his suspenders.

"Go get Lucy and Everett up," Mama said.

Ellie tiptoed past Everett, not yet able to face him. She walked loudly down the hall, past the boys' room, where they were already getting dressed.

"Lucy," Ellie said at their bedroom door. "Time to get up."

Lucy rolled over and opened her eyes, smiled and stretched her arms.

"Is he still here?"

Ellie nodded. "Mama will have breakfast ready soon." She walked down the hall and through the living room. Everett was pulling on his shirt.

"Guess I'll go see what's wrong with the car," he said loudly, not looking at Ellie. She wondered if she had dreamed last night.

As soon as everyone was settled around the long table, Daddy asked Everett to say the blessing. Lucy joined with an overly loud "amen" when the prayer was over. Mama looked at Daddy and smiled. Ellie took her time eating bacon. She wanted to get that butterscotch taste out of her mouth.

Daddy asked Everett about the car.

"Looks like a spark plug worked loose. Seems to be running

smooth now," Everett said.

Ellie kept her head down and ate.

After breakfast, Ellie helped Mama with the dishes. Daddy went out to look over the car with Everett while Lucy folded the sheet on the couch.

"Lucy, why don't you get dressed for church and ride to town with Everett?" Mama said. Lucy retreated to the bedroom, humming.

Ellie stayed in the kitchen, trying to find extra things to do. "You're awfully quiet this morning," Mama said. "You feeling okay?
"I'm okay."

Mama shook her head.

Soon, Lucy came into the kitchen. "How do I look?" She twirled around so her cotton eyelet skirt billowed out.

"Lovely," Mama said, "now get out of here. We'll see you and Everett at church. Ellie, you and I gotta get ready."

At church, Ellie scrambled out of the wagon along with her brothers. Mama carried Bess with her into the women's group in one of the back rooms of the church. Daddy went to the room where the men met, and Ellie and the boys went to a large room where the children sat on quilt pallets on the floor or in old church pews at the back. Ellie took a spot on one of the back pews, wanting to hide from Mrs. Hunt, the Sunday School teacher. She didn't feel up to Bible study. How could she sing "Jesus Loves the Little Children," or talk about God's love when she was still thinking about Everett reaching under her panties.

After the Bible lesson, Mrs. Hunt dismissed the class. The older girls and boys gathered up their Bibles and ushered the younger ones out into the sanctuary. Ellie took her time, looking at the pictures tacked to the wall.

"Everything okay, Ellie?" Mrs. Hunt said.

"Yes, ma'am."

Ellie stood in the doorway to the sanctuary and looked for her parents. She saw Everett at the back of the church with a cluster of children. He ruffled little Jenny Barrett's blond hair; she put her hand out for a candy. He looked up at Ellie and smiled. Her heart ricocheted against her ribs. She took a deep breath, dropped her head and hurried to her father who stood near the front of the church with Johnny and Robbie. Ellie grabbed her father's hand and tucked herself in close to his long tall legs. Daddy looked down at her with questioning eyes.

When Mama arrived with Bess, Daddy led them to a pew halfway back. Ellie settled herself next to her brothers while Lucy went to a back pew with Everett where the young people sat. He glanced at Ellie and winked. Ellie shifted her gaze to her hands clenched in her lap.

The pastor settled himself at the pulpit and said, "Let us pray." Ellie closed her eyes and tried to listen to the prayer, asking God to be with them today as they read His word. But she could only think of Everett winking at her and of Jenny Barrett and her outstretched hand.

The pastor's wife led the congregation in "Blessed Assurance," one of Ellie's favorites. She usually sang the chorus at full voice because it made her happy. But Ellie just stared at the open songbook on her lap. Daddy glanced at her and raised his eyebrows. She shrugged tentatively.

Just before the sermon, Reverend Lindell said, "And now, I'd like to invite Everett McBride up here to the pulpit. Come on up, Everett."

Ellie could hear scuffling behind her. She closed her eyes. The pastor continued his introduction of Everett, "and here's a young man who came to us only a few years ago, became a part of this community, and now he's going on to serve the Lord. Everett, tell us about your calling."

Everett smiled at the congregation from the pulpit and her parents smiled back at him. Ellie twisted a corner of her dress into a knot and studied the spiraling creases it made. She listened, head down, as he told the congregation he had gotten the call to follow the Lord like the twelve disciples.

Suddenly, breakfast bacon flowed up into Ellie's mouth. She swallowed hard, but her stomach burned. She felt the fatty excess surge again. She leaned past her brothers and whispered, "Mama, I don't feel good."

Mama said, "Shhh."

"But, Mama—" Ellie pushed back another surge.

Daddy frowned. Mama whispered, "Go outside and sit under the tree. Go on, now." Mama turned back to listen to Everett.

Ellie was afraid to move. She didn't want to bring attention to herself, but her stomach continued to turn. She folded her arms across her abdomen and laid her head back against the pew.

Daddy stared at her, brows pulled together, eyelids narrowed. He looked up at Everett and then at her. "Go on," he said quietly.

Ellie slid out of the pew past Mr. and Mrs. Wilcox. Soft tears puddled against her nose and trickled into her mouth. She walked as quickly as possible toward the open door.

At the church doorway, a warm breeze grazed her sweaty forehead. The nausea subsided, but she could not stop the flow of tears. Ellie ran to the deep shade of the old live oak, its branches spreading out in a crazy quilt pattern, offering patches of dark and light. Ellie sat against the base of the tree, listening to the rhythm of the sermon inside and the contrapuntal buzz of the insects in the pasture next to the church. Down the road she saw rows and rows of blackened cotton plants tufted with white dots. Eventually, she dozed.

"Eleanor, you all right?" Daddy's hand rested on her shoulder. She nodded yes, and he helped her to her feet. "Let's go," he said and led her to the wagon.

On the way home, Ellie sat in the back of the wagon up against the buckboard while the boys sprawled out on the wagon bed. Over her shoulder, Ellie could hear Mama's small talk with Daddy about the sermon. She finally mentioned Everett's announcement. "I'm glad he's made a public commitment. Maybe it won't be all talk now."

Daddy looked at Mama and then back at the road without saying anything. Mama continued, "Lucy thinks she's got a good one. I hope so. That girl wants to be married in the worst way."

"Uh-huh." Daddy slapped the reins at the mule.

"And she'll make a good preacher's wife. She works hard, sews well, everybody likes her. What are you gonna do if he comes askin'?"

"Say yes, I guess. But they're just as likely to go to a justice of the peace. That's how it is with young people in these automobiles. Let's hope she doesn't do anythin' foolish."

"Yes, let's hope," Mama said.

Ellie leaned her head over the wagon railing, cooling her face in the slight breeze as the mule clopped along.

At home, Mama told Ellie that she didn't have to help with Sunday dinner. "Go lie down for a while."

In the bedroom, Ellie listened to the low murmurs of Mama and Daddy on the other side of the house with occasional outbursts from the boys or the nonsense babbling of Bess. She drifted into sleep.

Ellie woke to soft whimpering. In the half-light of dusk, she saw Lucy sitting on the bed across the room. Her head bowed, she sobbed gently.

What's the matter, Lucy?"

"Nothin', nothin' at all." Lucy got up and turned her back to Ellie.

"You all right?"

"I'm fine." Lucy washed her face in the basin on the corner

stand. "Go on back to sleep."

She dried her hands, straightened her dress, stood up straight, smiled, and walked out of the bedroom.

Ellie heard Mama ask, "Ellie awake?" But she couldn't make out Lucy's reply. She stiffened when she heard Everett say, "Guess the heat got to her."

Ellie strained to hear the rest of the conversation, but the adults spoke too softly to be understood. After a while, the screen door creaked, a car motor turned over, caught and rattled away.

Mama came to the doorway. "How you feeling, hon?"

"I'm okay."

"You hungry? We've got some ham, cream peas and fried okry. I could make you a plate."

"What's wrong with Lucy?"

"Why, I don't think anythin's wrong with Lucy. She's just in a fever 'cause she's been with Everett. Why do you ask?"

"No reason."

"So can I fix you somethin'?"

"No." Ellie turned onto her side.

"Okay, you rest now. Daddy needs you in the field bright and early tomorrow. Just be sure you say your prayers before you go to sleep."

Late that night, Ellie heard her parents arguing in the living room. She couldn't make out the words, but she could hear Mama's soft entreating singsong alto and Daddy's bass punctuation. Lucy lay on the bed weeping.

"I will not allow it in this house," Daddy's voice boomed.

Again, Mama's soft tones floated into the bedroom.

"What's goin' on?" Ellie said.

"None of your business," Lucy said into her pillow.

Daddy walked heavily down the hall. Ellie got up from her bed and stood in the doorway. Daddy came out of his and Mama's bedroom carrying his shotgun.

"Daddy, you're not going hunting on a Sunday night, are you?"

"Noooooo!" Lucy screamed and ran toward the hall. Her nightgown twisted and caught at her knees, and she fell hard onto the wood planking. Bess began to cry.

"No, Henry!" Mama shouted from the end of the hall, her face white. "Henry, you can't do this. Lucy will never marry if you do."

Daddy looked from Mama to Lucy to Ellie, his jaw set like a ridge of granite exposed in the hillside, his high forehead a steep cliff colored with iron oxide.

The boys scrambled to the doorway of their bedroom, rubbing their eyes. Bess wailed in the corner crib while Lucy wept on the floor.

"Go on, shoot him!" Ellie wanted to scream. "Shoot him because he's a sinner of the worst kind." But she stood frozen against the doorframe, remembering Everett's hand on her thigh, reaching into her private place.

Daddy opened the gun, removed the two shells, and put them in his pocket. Closing the gun, he said to his wife, "I won't shoot him, but, by God, he will marry this girl."

He strode out of the house and Mama slid down to the floor. Lucy sobbed face down, her arms covering her head.

"What's happening?" Robbie said.

"Nothin', go back to bed," Mama said. "Just a bad dream. Go to bed, Lucy, Ellie."

Ellie helped Lucy into bed; she rolled over against the wall and whimpered. Ellie took the boys by the hand to their room, and then came back into the hall and sat on the floor next to her mother.

"It's Everett, isn't it, Mama? It's Everett."

"He took advantage of Lucy. He has an unclean mind and can't control himself."

"I know, Mama, I know. He touched me. He touched me down there."

Mama looked at her with sunken gray eyes. "Oh, Ellie. Oh, Ellie." Her face darkened. "Don't ever tell your daddy," Mama said in a whisper. "Don't tell Henry. Don't tell anyone."

"But, Mama, if we don't tell, he'll keep doin' it."

"It won't do you no good to tell. It won't do Lucy no good." Her mother pushed a strand of hair out of her sad eyes. "Don't tell," Mama said.

Eleanor sat in her daughter's living room recliner. Sunshine streamed in through the open blinds. Her twenty-year-old granddaughter, Amanda, leaned over and touched her knee. "So what happened, Grandma?"

Eleanor's small watery brown eyes looked up from the arthritic hands cradled in her lap, her fingers as gnarled as late-season boll spurs. Her thin white hair floated around her face like cotton fibers wafting off a wagon on its way to the gin.

"What happened? They married soon after. He eventually got a church and they had four kids, with the first comin' early—everybody said that happens sometimes with new mothers. Still, they changed churches every four years or so. I don't know if God helped him tame his appetites. Maybe Lucy did."

"But Grandma, why didn't you go to the authorities?"

Eleanor looked down at her hands and ever so slightly shook her head. "It was a different time, Amanda."

"But Grandma—"

"Amanda—" The old woman looked up fiercely at her granddaughter, her eyes hard and defensive. "I'll tell you why. 'Cause Mama said not to. 'Cause it would be a shame on the family, that's why." She looked down at her knotted hands. "'Cause no one would believe a twelve-year-old tomboy against a man of the cloth," she said quietly.

Eleanor shook her head. "I don't know if she was right. I don't know if tellin' could have saved some poor child from his sinful touch. But I never told anyone else—until now. God forgive me.

"Your mother always wondered why we didn't visit Aunt Lucy and Uncle Everett. Now you know why, and why I won't go to his funeral. I didn't care to see him in life. I don't need to see him in death."

She looked out the window at the manicured lawn of her daughter's suburban home. "Besides, it don't matter no more. They're all dead and gone," she said, her voice trailing off. "All dead and gone."

Ellie put a hand to her cheek and stared off into the past, remembering rows and rows of cotton stretching to the horizon, the heat of the late August sun, and the prick of dried black bolls in her bare palms. She also remembered the burnt taste of a hard butterscotch candy stuck against her tongue. She swallowed hard and sighed. "I'll take an ice tea now," she said.

Lucinda Trew

Carolina Clay

Earth beneath my home-tired feet
sinks,
casting footprints
shallow graves.

They say it heals, this ruddy mud
that chokes my step,
swallows my trail.

They say, they swear
that early tribes
once plastered snake bites,
poulticed burns
and purified lost
tainted souls.

They claim there's alchemy
in this loamy mire.
Soothed by a potter's touch,
baptized
by cleansing licks of flame,
the clay transforms.

Caressed and tempered
it holds a fine salt glaze,
cool spring water,
the rain
of where we come from.

Parched,
I crave more still –
more than the humble earth
that stains my skin
and pages,

more than the blessings
on my tongue.

I walk on –
and will my words
to dry and fly
like kiln-baked wings
in a cloud of dust.

Katherine Wolfe

Pears in Winter

The first Christmas
my sister was in California,
Palo Alto, she sent pears,
a dozen, each wrapped
in gold paper,
Royal Riviera Pears
for me in North Carolina.
Instructions were to let
the pears sit and ripen
further before eating.
During the ripening,
I thought of our North
Carolina grandmother's
pear tree in a field where
my mother said there
once was cotton,
a field where in summer
my sister and I played
and gathered hard, green
pears to take to Grandmother.
She let them ripen too
while we two sat in awe
waiting for the pear
preserving to begin.

Don Johnson

The Bug

As I was washing my hands in the bathroom, I noticed a small black dot moving across the sink. It was a tiny bug. Quite naturally I went to squish it, but as my thumb hovered over it, it seemed to react with fear. Can a tiny black bug know fear? I hesitated to squish it, and it went on its way. Did it have purpose? Was it hungry and seeking food? Was it looking for a mate? Does it have a sex drive? Does a tiny black bug have a sex drive? Unthinkable! Yet if it's species goes on, it must. I realized that that tiny black bug was actually a very complex being. Why was I so quick to want to squish it? Learning? Habit? Perhaps because some bugs, like mosquitoes, attack us, we lump them all together and squish them all without thinking. That's easier than seeing them as different from each other. But does that give us the right to squish such a complex creature?

All this because I went to wash my hands.

David E Poston

Pollen Angels

Not fallen, not those rebels
who haunt this broken world
like April's yellow pine scourge
tinting windshields and
scumming the edges of puddles.

We woke to flakes of snow
thick as muffins,
one day too late to be a joke,
but we couldn't resist imagining
the joys of snow cream,
snowmen,
walking hand in hand
down muffled streets
throwing snowballs
at each other and then
brushing the snow from
each other's hair.

Then I thought it cute
to take the sled down
from its rusty nail
and out to the sloppy driveway,
but of course that's just when
our daydreams melted into spring drizzle.

No snow angels today, we said,
yet we laughed even more
at the expense of the poor sled
lying there on the muddy grass
because nothing
takes away our joy these days.

David Dixon

The Nature of Leaves

In the deep fall
  don't you imagine the leaves think how
comfortable it will be to touch
    the earth instead of the
nothingness of air and the endless
    freshets of wind?   Mary Oliver

I am not the first to consider
    the nature of leaves and might they
        praise the faithfulness of stem
            to branch to trunk to root

while still the spirit free? Or
    do they shimmer and quiver,
        tremble and quake in the
            presence of some invisible lord?

Or others — perhaps lighter in heart —
    wave to all sides of the way with
        the flirtatious gestures of a beauty
            queen; or maybe some, I fancy

as timid and just a tad afraid of the
    height so that when you climb close
        they jump right in your
            pockets and follow you home

chattering gaily and singing
    the silly songs of Spring
        learned in the gentle lap of
            southern winds; although some

might implore your help for their
       sisters and brothers above who
            likely are most in apprehension
                  of the becoming of earth and

a welcoming of worms; but
       surely there are a chosen few
            who recognize the entire proposition
                  as the consecration of flight, the

abiding glory of not being given to a
       higher birth until we release all that to
            which we adhere, and the blessing of being
                  just as we are chosen — not at all like those

who remaining so unfallen — never learn to fly

Jenny Bates

Walking Stick, Walks Alone

Stick insect on a twig. L
                 O
                      N
                            G

legs rigid on velvet leaves.
Camouflaged codes never broken for millennia. Life without
discontent.

Worlds L
       O
            N
               G
                    E
                         S
                              T

insect knows things.
Who he is when hot weather comes. He can afford a bit of rest.

No commitments. It remains still.
      Patient. Meditative. Prayerful.
A dreamer for sure. Doesn't panic. Dreams of nothing. Eats his way
through ancient
Oak leaves. Stamps them like a butter-print. Secret love notes sent
to Theophrastus.

      Never too public. Too open. Too trusting.

           Strength through silence.

Teyako Bolden

Fighting for the Motherless

Chapter 1

I was in the third grade, attending my first Girl Scout meeting when I realized my family was different. For the first time I got asked the questions I would come to hate, *"where is your mom,"* *"where does she live,"* and the most popular *"why don't you live with her?"* As I think back on that time, I find it humorous they never asked me about my dad. Maybe it's okay for dads to walk away. I decided I needed a good story. At eight-years-old, that story was elaborate and changed constantly. To the girls in my troop I would brag constantly about my mom, *"She works for Universal Studios"* I would say *"we get free tickets to Disney World every summer."* Fast forward to middle school, the lies still came, but so did an acceptance on my part. I realized this was the hand life had dealt me. I'm old enough now to understand how lucky I was, not every child whose parents abandon them have a chance at the life I had. As for the lies, I crafted one more, it would be the last lie I would tell about my mother. She was no longer in far-off cities on grand adventures. To anyone who asked, the story was simple, *"my mom died when I was little, I don't even remember her."* It would be the first lie to hold some truth because she could be dead. In a way this was the lie to help twelve-year-old me face the reality of my circumstances, my mother was not coming back.

Chapter 2

My sisters and I were never close; still, to this day we have little in common. I'm not sure the reasoning, but from the beginning, they separated us. They sent my two oldest sisters to live with my great-grandmother; I remained with my grandmother and Aunt. Eventually, as we got older, my sisters became too much for my great-grandmother to handle and came to live with my grandmother and me. I must admit, not once have I ever stopped to put myself in their shoes. They bounced around from home to home, while I ended up with stability. I wonder what made me so special. Things were awkward at first, though they knew us and we knew them. We weren't distant relatives; we were sisters, but in the beginning that bond wasn't there. It took time. I was a bratty seven-year-old who didn't want to share her room. I can still remember all the times I got my second oldest sister in trouble. The worse being the time I carved the first three letters of my name into the kitchen wall and blamed her for it. I can't believe I got away with that one. Eventually, despite it all, a relationship formed. My oldest sister became my protector. She battled playground bullies and paid for book fair splurges. She had the biggest heart, but the shortest temper, like a live volcano, ready and waiting to erupt. Our home environment hurt. The reigns were always tight, almost to the point of suffocation, smothered in religion by my aunt. Discipline was second nature, because, as the good book says "spare the rod, spoil the child." Big Sis always got it the worse. Determined to live her own life, her own way, no matter the consequence. The worst was the night she snuck out and got caught. I still carry some guilt for the chain of events that occurred. A late night trip to the bathroom and an unlocked bedroom door would change the course of our lives. When my aunt came into our room to put away some laundry, she realized my sister snuck out. She waited, ready to hand out a punishment unbefitting of her crime. There were no talking things out with my grandmother and my aunt, no getting to the root of the problem. God knows we had enough problems to last a lifetime. Forever burned in my mind are the events of that night. The sound of an extension cord ripping through flesh intermixed with my sister's cries. I remember wanting to jump in front of her, to be her protector for once. I was too afraid. The last sounds I remember hearing that night were her muffled sobs and her small voice asking me to sleep with her. I was too afraid to even give her that. My oldest sister wouldn't last another year in our home. At fifteen she ran away, it would be months before we would hear from her. Another disappearing act, but the memory of this one wouldn't be blocked out.

My middle sister was a wild child, a real live carbon copy of my mother. It was my grandmother's greatest fear come to life. Early on they diagnosed her with hyperactivity. My sister is the first person I've ever known to take on Ritalin. My grandmother didn't know how to deal with her, my aunt didn't know how to deal with her, hell sometimes I didn't know how to deal with her. She was a live wire, always restless. A perfect example is a night she stole and wrecked our neighbor's station wagon. They could not control her, as a kid it was scary, even today it still is. Like my mother, my middle sister doesn't think about the consequences of her actions, or how her choices will affect others. The same demons that controlled my mother now control her. The similarities are eerie. The only difference is my sister is constantly at war within herself to not become our mother. She knows what kind of life her children could end up with if she does. When she fails, which she does, a lot, she picks herself up and readies herself for another battle; she keeps fighting. That's all any of us can really do.

Chapter 3

My story is a little different, a little more timid, than theirs. Where my sisters were bold with their choices, I played by the rules. I was afraid to make mistakes. I wanted to break the cycle. I would not be Marlana Bolden's daughter. I knew what the rest of our family said about us. They thought of us as a product of our environment. Apples never fall far from their trees. My mother didn't amount to anything, my sisters didn't amount to anything, so, surely I, the youngest of our brood, wouldn't amount to anything. My goal in life wasn't to live for me; it was to prove them wrong. I busted my butt during high school, determined to walk across that stage, but then my plans derailed. Two things would happen that would change the course of my life. The first was the return of my mother. The second was the death of my grandmother.

"She isn't dead." Those were my only thoughts upon hearing the news that my mother was in contact with members of our family. She was looking for us. She wanted to come home. Eighteen is already a tough age for any teenager, you are now an adult, tasked with planning out a direction for your life. The last thing you need is for an absent parent to make an appearance. I immediately decided I wouldn't have anything to do with her. I was an adult, I survived this long without a mother, her presence was no longer wanted or needed. Enter the game changer. We were no longer a trio, we were a quartet. I had a baby sister placed in the state of Illinois foster care system. Like it or not, I had little choice but to let this stranger into my life. Her first visit home in almost ten years was the evening before my high school graduation; my little sister wasn't with her, my mother unable to travel out of state with her. Her visit served me no purpose, and I refused to share this moment with her. She had no right to be there, she didn't deserve to watch a child she abandoned accomplish a thing. The closer the time of her arrival got, the more irrational I became. I yelled at my grandmother in complete hysterics. *"Why is she coming here now, why would you invite her to my graduation! No one even knows she exists."* I made threats *"If you invite her, I won't go, I won't walk."* The tears in my grandmother's eyes stopped me cold, she was a mother whose child had come home. I couldn't stand to be there any longer; I needed an escape, something to lose myself in. I called up some friends and minutes later I was drowning my thoughts in a bottle of vodka in a Motel 6 off of Ashley Phosphate Rod. This was the beginning of my spiral. We all have our demons, even if we don't know their names.

The death of my grandmother was the derailment that put me over the edge. I was barely nineteen. It was a stroke, what a simple word for something that can be so vicious to the body and mind. The first one went undetected, the second left her down for the count. It hit so hard and fast, like a hurricane through the Florida panhandle, with no time to prepare. I put my life on hold to take care of her; it was only fair she had done the same for me. My grandmother required round-the-clock care, she couldn't walk, talk or eat by herself. It was just her and me in that house. My daily routine consisting of administering medication, changing adult diapers, stretching out arms and legs and providing feedings through a G-tube. I was lonely and depressed, no longer able to maintain a social life; her care consumed my world, day and night. I wasted all of my efforts; I wasn't enough. Her condition worsened, the only option was to place her in the care of a nursing home. We decided and for the second time in my life; I lost myself in another bottle, the numbness ever so addicting. I failed her. My grandmother wouldn't last a full year in that nursing home. She died three days before my twenty-first birthday. After her funeral I needed out of Summerville, I needed to be somewhere else, be someone else. I planned my escape.

Chapter 4

I thought moving to Charlotte was what I needed. It was my chance to become someone new, to stop being the good girl that took care of everyone and everything. I could forget. So many bottles, so little time. At the bottom of one, I will find happiness. This wasn't too far from the truth. A year into my new life, I was at the bottom of one of those bottles and low and behold, nine months later I found happiness. Accompanied by the realization, I was my mother's daughter. I had become the thing I was running from. I struggled with this new identity. "How could I make the same mistakes?" This was the question constantly haunting my thoughts. I became terrified at the direction I was heading. I didn't know how to steer myself back on course. July 4, 2007, was the day it all fell into place. The moment the nurse placed that gorgeous little girl on my chest I could feel some darkness and uncertainty releasing its hold on me. I cried, muttering repeatedly *"she is so beautiful, I can't believe she is mine."* Nothing else in this world mattered. I didn't need to have all the answers; I just needed to have the want to be better. That's all I could ask of myself. I had a purpose and this little girl was it, I wanted her to have all the securities, I only dreamed of having in life. It won't be easy, nothing in life worth having ever is. As for my mother and me, my love for my baby sister has broken through some barriers. Not all, the scars are still there and on the days when they reopen, I have two amazing little girls who don't mind helping to stitch them up.

Jeanne Julian

The Dead Woman's Suitcase

My husband brings it home for me.
Basic black, good condition.
Cardboard I.D. tag looped unfaded
on the handle: Mrs. McIntyre.
A damp sponge does the trick,
wiping away slight trace of her
household's final dust resting
faintly on the top. Inside, immaculate.
One-year warranty and desiccant packet
still tucked neatly in a pocket.
No forgotten nail clippers, no toothpaste smear.
No strand of hair to betray her
fastidiousness, or to suggest her looks,
her age. Her modesty remains
intact, as at a closed-casket funeral.

Where did Mrs. McIntyre go
with her tidy quilted roll-aboard?
No lingering grains of Bermuda sand,
no Broadway ticket stubs, no pink-crowned
wrapper from a Bruyerre Belgian chocolate.
Imagine Mrs. McIntyre at Wimbledon!
Soaking in Seljavallalaug hot spring pool!
Mrs. McIntyre blushing in Bhutan
at phallus images decorating houses!
Like a blank book this empty emissary,
transferred from one crammed closet
to another, calls out "Fill your life, now!"
as we wonder:
where did Mrs. McIntyre go
without her suitcase?

Joyce Compton Brown

The Doctor Sends Martha Mason on an Iron Lung Odyssey in Lattimore, North Carolina
(1936-2009)

When she was eleven
he told her she would die quite soon,
to use the lens of death's bright focus
to saturate the weeks with life's intensity.
When pulsing bellows stopped, she'd be
renowned for giving her parents joy
to carry to their journey's end.

They shipped her small self
to homebound death in slow rhythm,
breath drawn in and out by bright yellow machine,
massive metal lung encircling inert small body.
They rolled her to her place, past the church,
up the ramp, to the room where little dog
leapt for joy and kissed her dangling hand.

She'd live beyond the designated weeks,
the months into years, always the sucking air,
the long slow hiss, the body gaining mass,
the small head still free, the mind leaping,
pushing hard against encapsulating lung,
against the room, against mirrored faces,
awkward smiles, and homecooked platitudes.

The books came, neighbors turned pages.
Mouth held pencil, screens began to shine,
flashing through more worlds than most
would ever see, the mind in motion sixty years,
three pounds of grey matter against atrophy
in Lattimore. Always the slow pant, the slow release,
the mind climbing out and out till iron lung's last breath.

Susan Alff

Custody

I am cowbird. Make of me what you will
depending on the credos of your kind
I drop my egg into your nest. All hell
breaks loose. You rage, entombing yours and mine
Maybe you're so harried you won't notice
What's one bird more or less amid the din?
Changeling--*need need need*--will find his solace
He's first to fill his gullet.
                            Mother, lend
your heart to this rough intruder, Other
My chick, your charge, he soon enough will flee
and perch on the rim of the worn ruined world
fly from nurture to knowing, and home to me
    I cannot shake my nature or the past
    Still, I teach the sweet chimes, sing the long grass.

Glenna Hurlbert

If It's 11:15 It Must Be Bedlam

"My baby," my mother lights up to say on some days when I walk into her room at the care center, but she cannot hold that thought. My heart rises and leaps only to plunge again when her affect goes flat and she closes her eyes in resignation. Back down her own hole in the universe, she dives, where she is young and on the family farm with her mother and sister.

I, as her surviving child, her legal representative, am enmeshed in her business. I flew in from North Carolina to prepare for an estate auction, the aftermath of Mother leaving her home. Mother and I are very close, but since she broke her hip, I haven't been able to be with her every day. A couple of times this week, when I stopped by to see her, she was sleeping. I didn't wake her primarily because I come away undone every time I try to help her into the present. My proud mother of the colorful fashion-forward, of the always alert and informed crowd, is now reduced to a faint echo of her history.

It is lunch time when I arrive today. I forget how early they serve meals. I'm self-conscious as I walk across the dining room — many eyes are upon me in speculation. Aides are slowly serving the independent eaters first. I look for Mother; she is not at her usual table. Then I spy her in the horseshoe of those patients who need help to eat. Mother sits there, detached from the clatter, in the line with six other residents.

My lovely mother, sans her chestnut curls and swinging ear bobs, is grey and diminished. In her washed-out denim robe she looks like a wary child caught in the heavy wheelchair. She's lost more weight recently, and her hair hangs white and lank. Her costume jewelry is in her bedside table for the duration.

I pull up a chair to sit beside Mother. She acknowledges me with a smile, but no recognition. Always mannerly, I think, even when there is little else left.

Abruptly, a woman who is two wheelchairs removed from Mother, sets her bare foot on her serving table and begins pounding her thighs with her fists, crying loudly,

"I wish, I wish, I wish. Oh, I wish."

The tiny woman who sits between the wishing woman and Mother jerks quick, bird-like glances to each side and responds,

"Whoo-oo, whoo-oo, whoo-whoop! Whoop!"

Her voice is long and drawn out on the "whoo"s, rising on the "whoop"s.

The plump man on the end grumbles. He mutters loudly, and fortunately, is unintelligible, because it sounds as though he's hurling curses at all of us. I sit stunned. I take deep breaths. Two days ago Mother had occupied her regular seat at an independent table.

I look around the room. No one seems to notice the behavior in the horseshoe - not aide or resident. As I look my eye fixes on the movement of a little woman sporting a pink fedora who is trying to get her wheelchair to her assigned table. She has miscalculated her path and cut in too close to a side table, catching her wheel on the table leg. She doesn't seem to recognize that she must back up, un-hook and go around it. She sits there stuck, pushing, working, urging her chair forward when it isn't about to leave the table onto which it has latched. The young aides pass her by without a glance, their hands full of food trays.

One of the aides comes and speaks to the woman who is still "I wish"-ing and striking herself.

"Virginia, please take your foot off your table, we need to serve your food."

Virginia pauses for a moment as though considering this, but doesn't change anything. The woman next to her is still "whoo-whoo"-ing. This commotion finally penetrates Mother's haze. She cuts her eyes side-ways at me, smiles sweetly, and whispers,

"Cra-zee."

I'm immobilized, emotionally frozen. I try to think of some way to help someone. The woman caught on the table across the room has disappeared into the crowd. I glance at Mother. She's dozing in her chair, still waiting for her meal. I've had all I can take for one day. I don't hang around to see what Virginia does with her foot.

David Dixon

Convenient

What kind of person notices the retirement
community centered between the funeral
home on one side and the cemetery on the
other and considers how they are not in proper
order as one is passing from either direction

and how it could be awkward on check in day
when you drop off the old man and have to
say Dad we know you'll like it here but try not
to look to the right nor the left as we get out of
the car and could we have a room with a view
straight out the back or even facing the traffic.
Even a small one will do as dimensions are no
concern for those so eager to empty as if by
merely cutting loose so many bags of sand
                    we could steady and rise

So is also the person waiting for absolution.
Having so comfortably within reach on the final
day of dispossession — the last two things
                    I'll need

Joanne Durham

Tribute to Mary Oliver (1935-2019)

She reminds you gently of your place
inside the world's tenderness.
Her flight like that of the butterfly

yes, this butterfly, that landed nearly
in your lap in this quiet space
carved from your crowded day,
beating her urgent translucent wings
across this meadow
from purple coneflowers to creeping phlox,
sipping nectar
where the wingless or impatient
would never find it,
then disappears down a dusty path

lost to the tiny range of your human eye,
but not the expansiveness
of your human heart.

Jenny Bates

Middle Earth

And I slip just like the stars into obscurity... —
Tom Waits

The day my mother and I painted my room sea-foam green I should have vowed never to leave home.

She wants me to be like my dull friend Bonnie, who somehow she knew would *do the right thing,* and stay. Stay, take care of her parents later in life. Mom was right about Bonnie. She was right about a lot of things. Comfortable in middle class suburbia, I listened, but did not believe her. I had — an everything-future.

I was in middle school, Clara Barton Jr. High, Royal Oak, Michigan. My best friend Diana, *her mother dated my father in their youth,* had knee length blond hair framing a pre-Raphaelite oval, pale blue eyes, skin like cream. The kind of face medieval knights would joust over. We would listen to Beethoven on her porch wearing flower patterned halter dresses, read **The Hobbit** and **Lord of the Rings** by lamplight. Our world was adventurous, awash in the colors of Rivendell.

Later in life, I would see Diana again in the dark recesses of Detroit's music scene. She sang lead in a punk-rock band. That flowing hair shaved, cut boy-short. Her skin aged, tattooed. After the concert, in a chic gallery next door I called her name. She did not recognize my voice as it must have trailed over her four foot head. I'm not tall, but I was shocked she never grew much past sixth grade. As her eyes shifted up to mine with recognition, she embraced me with a hug I still feel. One you learn throughout life means, *don't let go.*

She left her head cradled in my shoulder like a sleep-over. No words or time passed between us. In that grimy, smoke filled room shadows melted into shadows. Shining eyes lit fading worlds that felt too grown-up for our wanderings. We were back in Middle Earth. After a moment, she slipped away. Drunken laughter cleared the air, Diana disappeared into the crowd. Our friendship finished, like the gentle closing of a good book.

Sam Barbee

Appearances

Palette, pentimento, chiaroscuro
discipline and dignity with stained fingers
swatches across white smocks, long shirts.

Noble and soothing, grace notes
adagio, intermezzo, fortissimo
gut-wrench beauty on breath, against reed.

Estrange alter-ego. luminous idioms
iamb, trochee, stumbling spondee
rising or falling, brazen while inviolate.

Legibility, fused volatility, scuttle
of reticent ghosts, surfacing in the moment
on the monument – the innocents.

The Real Thing, King of Beers, favorite Red or Rosé
all guzzled and pissed away
found their place with the other saints.

Reformation, Inquisition, Blessing the Animals
each pivot a flair, brings us back: reclaim the dead
limbo, purgatory, third-day stroll.

Re-do, pump with pomp
each sun a star: star flares someone's wish –
every moon a plea: moon convenes wane.

Jenny Bates

Opus Dei — a trinity of conviction

I

Leonardo da Vinci

pissed me off.
Please, let poetry be more than contemplating the Renaissance
space between your navel and your legs. You are not the center
of the universe. Shock. I know.

II

Louis-Ferdinand Celine

is a vampire...
The point of poetry is to stir you like a recipe. Educate you like a baby
bird in a nest. Stick to your tread like mud, so you have to dig it out,
hose it off to be rid of it. Full of new things — and holes, and holes.
The soul doesn't care, but poetry washes your courage, wishes, luck.

III

When poetry is your church, then make our words the work of your God.
Walk the vertical Thomas Beckett nave of your intelligence. Sit in the
Martin Luther pews of your heart. Cross with crosses, stigmata in the
Francis of Assisi apse. Pace is grace to the sick, the poor, the animals.

IV

Diogenes

was right.
Nothing will be left of your baggage. Only a lantern held high not like
religion, but invention. If you don't understand, rethink it. Listen to
your dog. He may be the only one listening to you. There is a reason
they call it dogma. No difference in kind, only in degree. I'm not
asking for doctoral stages, notches or grades. Try to be as smart as
a tree. Dog pee on your poetry. Grow up.

Janet Joyner

Now Come Hyacinths

their slender blue lath erect
and reeking of perfume
in the shortening of dark
and the lengthening day.
It is the time of blurry lines
when winter silhouettes
of trees grow fuzzy,
when nests reappear,
and maples first submit
limb tips to fresh hints
of brownish-red morphing
daily into reddish–brown
before settling down into
muted claret, or soft pastels
previewing the autumnal flame;
when the Bradford pear
fluffs out those puffs
of white, inevitable match
for flakes of occasional
late snow; or when the cherry
tree's audacious pale pink
foreshadows forsythia's rush
to beat the daffodils to gold.
This is the time to marvel
once again at the turning,
the gravitational yearning
for the light, far flung
and awed as we are,
that any of this,
any of us
still here…are.

Allison Hong Merrill

Lightning Whisperer 與閃電的對話

Hualien, Taiwan. 1977

I talked to someone in the sky when I was four, and he talked back. Through lightning.

My family lived in a traditional Japanese house—a minka—that had been a government official's compound during the Japanese Occupation Era (1895-1945 A.D.). The kitchen was the only concrete space: concrete floor, concrete sink, concrete counter. One night, Mama put a white apron over her floral print dress to prepare dinner. My two-year-old sister, Dee, and I sat behind her on the dining room wood floor, drawing houses and stick people on old newspapers. Soon, the cold concrete space was filled with rhythmic chopping on the cutting board, the hissing sound of boiling water pushing against the pot lid, the sizzling sound of washed vegetables tossed into an oil-heated pan. I inhaled deeply for what came next: the explosive fragrance of fried garlic mixed with pork, carrots, and cabbage. And then, the mild scent of chicken and shitake mushroom soup. There was fried rice with ham and egg, too. The soup steam created beads of sweat on the window glass above the stove, distorting the amber sunset lights slanted through.

When Mama arranged the fresh dishes on the dining table, I held up Dee so she could see the dinner. "Don't drool all over the food," I told her. Mama slapped me on the arm with her greasy hand. "Don't you pick anything off the plate now. Wait for Baba to come home. Then we eat."

Mama sat at the table, Dee and I at her feet. My stomach grumbled. Dee fell asleep. Around nine o'clock, past our bedtime, Baba staggered in the door, his eyes bloodshot, his breath an alcoholic sour stink. He wobbled over to the dining table, wordlessly surveying the now-cold food, and spewed curses. "YOU CALL THIS SHIT DINNER?"

With one wild swing of his arm, he swept everything off the surface and flipped the table. Mama's culinary creation, along with chopsticks and ceramic bowls, flew in the air. All of it scatter-landed on the floor.

He grabbed Mama's hair, pulling and twisting and making her head tilt at an unnatural angle. As if deaf to her plea for mercy, he slammed her face against a wall, over and over, creating a bloody hole in the wall the shape of a heart. He turned our home into a battlefield. Turned Mama's begging cry into an injured-animal howl. Turned my stomach-growling-hunger into stomach-churning-terror.

Dee screamed and ran into our tatami bedroom, finding shelter behind the shoji rice-paper-sliding door. I was sure Baba would hurt me too if he saw or heard me, so I crawled toward a mound of shoes by the door and crouched, hoping to be out of his sight. But that didn't stop my pounding heart from threatening to break out of my chest. I pinched my lips to stifle the ready-to-erupt wail in my throat.

Mama broke away from Baba's demonic grasp and threw a chair at him. Her face and teeth were covered in blood, her white apron stained maroon. She yelled at him, but I couldn't make out her words, or if she spoke his native Hokkien or her native Hakkanese. More things flew across the room from either side of where they were fighting: table lamp, plates, teapot. Their shadows on the broken wall were like shadow puppetry, unfolding the horror tale of my shattered family.

Mama left after the fight that night, leaving Dee and me with Baba in the ruins. Looking back, I know now that during my parents' nineteen years of marriage, Mama lived with a packed suitcase, always ready to leave him and go back to her parents. She needed her parents when she was emotionally injured. But she must have not thought I needed her when I witnessed domestic violence.

Baba went to work the next morning. I woke up on the concrete kitchen floor, among slippers, flip flops, sandals, scattered morsels of food, shards of ceramic bowls, broken chairs. My stomach growled, my head felt light. I shooed away rats and fed Dee leftovers on the floor for breakfast. When I scooped up a handful of cabbage leaves and rice to make a ball, my eyes welled up, my nose tingled. The food in my palms looked blurry as I shoved it into my mouth.

Dee and I squatted by the front door, watching motorbikes on the street all day, waiting for someone to come home. Finally, Baba did. He put Dee on the fuel tank of his motorcycle, me behind him, and took us to the night market for dinner.

The night market was full of life. Street lamps and string lights over vendor booths made it as bright as daytime. Bustling crowds sat at folding tables by the roadside or squatted on the street by the gutter, eating chicken feet, pig's intestine vermicelli, pig's blood cake. Stray, diseased dogs with patches of missing fur, oozing pus, and chewed-off ears circled the booths, looking for crumbs on the ground. The air wafted with the aromas of barbeque corn on the cobs, steamed meat buns, salt-and-pepper deep-fried ribs. I wanted to eat everything in sight, especially roasted sausages with garlic, but Baba only ordered wanton noodle soup, roasted duck, and fried clam with basil.

Dee was a messy eater. Baba blow-cooled the food in his own bowl and spoon fed her, while sipping a can of Taiwan Beer. At home, he made us finish every single grain of rice in our bowl, it was no different in the night market. And I gladly complied. I was starving. Starving for food, for a peaceful home, for a loving family. In the ecstasy of enjoying street food, I momentarily forgot about Mama, about what Baba had done the previous night that led us here.

After dinner, Baba took us to his drinking buddy's house. As soon as Baba parked his motorcycle on the veranda, a group of men hollered at him, in Hokkien, from the living room. "Hey, Old Hong! Get in here!" Even through the iron roll-up door I could smell alcohol coming from inside the house. Baba shoved me in the back and said in Chinese, "Take Dee. Go play with other kids in there. I'm going to talk to my friends. Won't be long."

Even at age two Dee demonstrated the social skills of making quick friends, a gift that grows more substantial as she ages. Unlike me, in a crowd of strangers she will never be alone. This night at Baba's drinking buddy's house, she plowed over the pony-sized sleeping dogs on the living room floor and toddled toward the sounds of laughing, playing kids, while I stood by Baba's motorcycle, sucking my right thumb and waiting to leave.

The weather worsened. I jumped at the deafening sounds of a thunderstorm with downpours of rain. I don't remember now how long I waited for Baba. I don't remember, either, what made me wander down the street. Probably the lightning. The lightning flashed in intervals. One second there were bright streaks slicing through the dark sky, one second they were gone. It looked like there was a room in the sky where the lights were turned on and off, on and off.

Someone is up there playing with a light switch! I thought.

Soaked and shivering, I was alone on an empty street, on the marble sidewalk that seemed to have turned from its black-and-white pattern into glue, sticking to my feet so I couldn't move. I stood there, marveling at the mysterious beauty of lightning.

"Is someone up there?" I asked, as if speaking with a tall person hovering over me.

Lightning

Oh, oh, oh, that's a yes! That's a yes! Someone is really up there!

"Rains are coming down from the sky. Are you wet?"

Silence

That's a no, that's a no!

"Do you live in the sky? In a home with a roof?"

Lightning

Hmmm, what does a house in the sky look like? What's it like to live so close to thunder?

"Are you scared of thunder?"

Silence

No? So brave.

"Do you know my name?"

Lightning

He knows my name? Wow!

"Are you alone, like me?"

Silence

There're more people up there!

"Can you see me?"

Lightning

He can see me! Of course he can. He's way up there, he can see everything and everyone—

Just then it hit me. If this person could see everyone, then he could see Mama too.

Mama—

I wondered if she was still bleeding and howling. I wondered if she had a nice dinner in the night market too . . .

"Do you know where my mama is?" I asked the person in the sky. "She left—"

Lightning

He knows where Mama is! He can see her. Yes! I clapped and cheered. *He knows where Mama is!*

The person in the sky was a giant. He must be. Otherwise he wouldn't be able to reach into the cloud. If he was a giant, then he must have a giant brain. And because he had a giant brain he must *know* everything. There was just one more thing I wanted to ask . . .

"Is my mama ever coming home?"

On the tiny tropical island of Taiwan, in the fishing village of Hualien, a roaring thunder shook the ground, silencing all noises around me. Across the dark night sky, the most majestic, blinding lightning shoot out of the celestial dome, reaching into the end corners of the earth. In this moment I felt like the giant in the sky had reached down with long arms, cradling me and whispering with a calm, silvery voice, "Yes, child. She's coming home."

Instantly I burst out sobbing. I couldn't stop hiccup-crying. But as I did, the tense feeling that had been developing in my chest since my parents' fight gradually dissolved. The power of those words made me feel as if the rain had washed away all the hurt in my heart. As if all the wrongs in my home had been rectified. As if all the broken things and relationships had been mended. And it was now a new home. A safe haven. A peaceful place.

The next morning at home,

when I woke up,

when my tears had dried up,

Mama showed up.

Glenna Hurlbert

Heyday

Sears
"wish book"
was the name
we heard mostly.
The big book arrived
yearly in the mail. We
poured over it by lamplight
after supper on the farm. Its
bright cover was in color; pages
inside were sepia. We dog-eared leaves
we liked – a puzzle, paints, or shiny gewgaw
to pin on a dress collar, or a skirt we hoped
might swish as we swayed into Sunday School. We sniggered
at the corset and girdle section, the models corn-fed
American girls looking like someone's mother from our town.
We lingered over fox fur cuffs on a coat we imagined was
scarlet or Nile blue, and gasped at slick refrigerators we knew were
pristine white. We worked out Christmas lists from that catalog in mid-September.
By eight o'clock we'd hoarded enough dreams to soothe us to sleep on corn-husk mats
near the stove 'til Ol' Red crowed us awake to milk Bess and Doll before the bus honked.

JoAnn Hoffman

A Question of Vulnerability

I will never wear shoes again, sighs my eight-year old,
burrowing bare toes deeper into sun-hot sand,
except in winter, she amends.

Later, she runs ahead of us on the slick, packed sand
at the tide line, feet *slap-slapping* in the shiny wet,
the slight wounds left by her toes on the surface
soothed and removed by the next wave.

Why wear shoes indeed, I think, my own bare feet
relishing the cool wash of waves on my toes,
the tickle of spindrift exhaling past my ankles.

It's a question of vulnerability, I decide.
Even the child knows feet want warmth in winter.
Watching her joyful barefoot run, I imagine sharp stones,
rusty nails, broken bottles, dead fish, insects.

Protection, then. We protect our soft spots. With helmets,
gloves, band-aids. With knee pads, safety glass, sunscreen,
ear muffs, oven mitts. Shoes protect the vulnerable sole.

But what protection for our helpless hearts, that bruise in a
heartbeat,
carry sorrow like a millstone, fall into fire one day,
freeze over the next, that run headlong into hurt,
surprised by the sting, like the ambush of a jellyfish under sand.

We need a shoe for the heart. A shell-hard shoe to resist piercing,
lined with sherpa for warmth, with spongy cushions
for comfort. A slip-on that will never tie too tight.

That night I dreamed I saw heart shoes in a catalog online.
I was the old woman who lived in a shoe and bought dozens of pairs
for all my shoeless children, dismayed to find that not a single pair fit.

Chase Harker

The Mill

Percy dipped his cupped hands into the cool, valley stream––lifted them to his lips and sipped. Beneath his reflection he could see sunken water lilies. A school of reddened trout darted beneath the water's surface. Around him the Blue Ridge Mountains rose and fell in endless ranges, and rolled into a pale horizon tinted with varying shades of blue. Mount Mitchell—with its esteemed height––loomed like an overseer in the hazy distance; its peak entangled with high, unseen clouds. Lush greenery blanketed the landscape in every direction; the tips of yellow birch and white oak swayed with the wind.

The crystalline stream—which ran like a vein throughout the Appalachian range— connected all the villages of the region. Warm, spring zephyrs had brought melted snow down from the Appalachian peaks—which made the stream surge with a slighter intensity. The region (with the exception of its villages and inhabitants) held its quiet anonymity within the foliage of its enfolding mountainous terrain.

In the field of his father's—or rather his father's landowner, for he was a tenant farmer—Percy helped tend to crops. His physical build was slim, and his stature was long. He had a calm disposition, and his dull, blue eyes burned wildly and incessantly with curiosity.

Daybreak marked its descent with shadows which hung over the valley. Percy saw gazania daisies curl their petals unto themselves. He admired his native sunset—dashed with streaks of red, orange, and faint maroon—and decided to return to his family's cottage.

Familiar faces became visible once he reached his village; some greeted him with smiles. Two young girls holding dry, water pots strove cheerfully past him. He wondered what type of seed his family would sow for the spring. Tobacco had been planted the previous season, which meant the new crop would be a different kind. This technique kept the fields rich and fertile every year.

Percy walked the stone path which aligned with his front door, and his mother called out to him from a small barn adjacent to the house.

"Percy, my boy," she said, "your father has some wonderful news to tell you!"

"What is it, Ma?" Percy asked.

"It's about the farm," she said. "Go on in and hear for yourself."

Percy opened the cottage door and darted inside. He motioned toward the den, and called out for his father.

"One moment, son," his father said. "I have something to show you."

He heard his father's footsteps, and noticed an opened letter in his hand once he entered the den.

"You remember your friend John, don't you?" his father asked. "The boy who moved to Lincoln County? Take a look at this letter."

Percy's eyes scanned up and down the letter.

"Look where it's addressed from," his father said.

The bold heading of the letter read:

Lincolnton Cotton Mill

Lincoln County, North Carolina

"What does it mean, Pa?" Percy asked. "Is it John?"

"It's from Lincoln County, where John moved," his father said. "A job offering from that large cotton factory there. John and his family work there, and there's a whole wing dedicated to young boys like yourself.

"Oh yes!" Percy cried, his cheekbones raised with his smile. "When will we be going?"

"Early June," his father said.

"You sure that John is there?"

"As sure as anything."

"What about our fields?" Percy asked.

"Instead of tending to crops, we'll have them brought to us," his father said. "We'll learn to weave yarn and cloth from cotton, providing essentials for good people like us throughout the East."

The sun had completely set when his mother entered the cottage holding a wooden platter covered in greens and freshly-skinned turkey breast. The family ate their dinner with an elation of spirit, and after cleaning the table, Percy retired into his bed. Heavy-eyed and excited for the future, he drifted to sleep.

*   *   *

Startled awake and sweating profusely, Percy sat up-right in his bed. He had had a nightmare—a dark vision of some sort. He had been back at the stream. It was dawn, but nothing of the landscape stirred. The petals of the gazania daisies were still curled, and no dew had descended upon the grass. Percy walked the edge of the stream, and perceived it was stagnant. A cloud of confusion penetrated his mind. The world was completely silent. He listened for the songs of birds—which announce the coming of day—when out of the woodline, on the opposite bank of the stream from himself, emerged a human figure.

The figure motioned toward Percy, who was bound in a paralysis-induced terror. It rendered itself visible once closer, and to Percy's surprise it was his friend John.

"John!" Percy yelled.

The figure was silent.

"John! Can you see me?" he asked.

The figure moved closer.

Percy called out again, and perceived something was wrong: John was coughing and convulsing as if possessed by an illness.

Percy attempted to move, but was still bound where he stood. Sunbeams fell onto John's face and illuminated his features. He looked incredibly thin and pale—almost ghost-like. Percy noticed blood trickling from John's mouth. He collapsed into the stream, and it slowly commenced its flow. Percy screamed out for John as his dream faded to consciousness.

*   *   *

When Percy awoke it was midnight, and his mother and father were asleep. On his father's bedside table—beneath some spectacles and dimly-lit by the moon—the letter from Lincolnton Cotton Mill lie.

Miles away in Lincolnton, John laid in his bed, and watched the moon trace across the skyline through his window. He was hardly clinging to life—pale, thin, and shivering under his quilts—experiencing the final stages of Byssinosis.

Claire Scott

Balancing on Broken Nights

slow dancing with a cigarette
& a gas can
swaying on the street behind Mel's
synapses stripped raw
coked up & down
rolling white pills
like a rosary
wrestling better angels
in a halo of haze
Hail Mary shows up
she has had a few
or a few have had her
Lord lost her mind
or maybe that is me I
whatever me
pray for us sinners
facing an unfolded future
written like a manga book
right to left ruins
sirens, wrenched arms, cuffed wrists
Hail Mary slips away
no sigh of mercy
better angels tap out
a cop kronks my head
red stars & bars
slumped in the backseat
edges bleeding
is there still time
is there still
now and at the hour
of our death

Jessica Lindberg

Clocktower Pigeons

The day after we sunk your dad's bequest
into our first house in Rome, Georgia, the city

poisoned the Clocktower pigeons. They spread
pellets of Pest Rid on the marble ledge

below six o'clock, and by noon realized
their mistake. Worse than the slow drip of shit

from the tower were soft flumps on car hoods,
feet up, or their spasmodic flight patterns

as these toxic messages delivered
themselves as far away as Anniston.

The sheriff sent a flock of prisoners
to patrol the courthouse lawn, to observe

the sky, catch the small sandbags, as most birds
spiraled near home, their decrescendos

in time to the chimes of up so many
ringing bells down, sound waves on the hour
rippling the top film of the Oostanaula River.

Jenny Bates

30600 Hours shared with 36200 Plymouth Rd.

1942: my father's post-grad advisor at Purdue told him he'd never make as much money teaching philosophy, as he would on the assembly line. Dad was a professor sheathed in a 35-year factory job at Ford Motor Company, Livonia, Michigan. He taught me, *you live in a grand narrative wrapped in small achievements*. He read every book he could while running that tool & die machine. Turning pages as quick and easy as layering car parts. The rhythm of Detroit's industry became fluent as his pen used to be.

The plant mattered to him because his family did. Yet, at times I think the transition from college, to machine shop, to father of two hardly touched him at all. I never saw my dad as a line-man. Even so, he tooled his children as fine as steel bearings, so we would never die when life challenged us. To me he was astronomer, futurist. Always carried a picture of a 3-wheeled electric car — the *car of the future*, in his wallet.

He stopped writing. Getting home from work at midnight invaded the pages until they were left blank. Closed for the remainder of his life, though he retained a skilled and crafted vocabulary no earthquake could shake. He'd wash off his children's greasy variations with Lava soap and a laugh.

His voice could deliver Edgar Allen Poe's **To Helen**, 1925's **Tea for Two**, or a yell of *He's out!* in the stands of old Tiger Stadium. My dad had large labor hands — still, his right index finger took on a pause or gesture that belied his erudite ease. Steady and automatic as the transmissions he built. When he died, I held on to the fading elegance of that digit.

1968: *In my lifetime,* he'd say, *we went from the ox-cart to the moon.* We would sit out in the front yard, look through a telescope. My young cheek next to his stubble, as he smiled, introducing me to the big dipper and the moon. Bits of heaven visible under street-lit suburbia.

He was cheerful in the seat of a ballet at the Fisher Theatre, as on the tractor in the field of his family farm. Gritted and gritty, he could drive seven days a week in a straight line, on the same route, to the same job. Then fly in the family car over the hills of Hillman, foot on the *exhilerateor*, joyously dizzy as the car left the ground on hometown country roads.

Dad was a Blue-collar scholar. Never looked down upon any soul — reminding us, *oxen may give a different effort, but its no less valuable than a man.*

Janis Harrington

We Meet Our Guide at the Sedona Diner

where he and our brother kicked off camping trips
with buckwheat pancakes and coffee, their ritual.
Loss washing over his face, Ben steers us
to a vinyl booth, then regales us with their tales:
mysterious lights above a vortex, rattlesnakes,
sunset tequila. Never accepting second-best,
Nick brought chefs' knives, barista grinder, French press,
carafe, wine glasses…once, abandoned it all
to half-carry his friend, ankle broken, back down.
Ben raises a thick white mug, and we imagine
our brother, across from us, lifting his cup.
Outside, we prepare to hike to their special site.
Loyal pallbearer, Ben shoulders the backpack
with the box of ashes…one final trek.

Jesse Millner

Dreaming of Dead Baptists and Headhunters

Last night I dreamed I was walking
down a narrow country road
beneath stars and oak trees, when, suddenly, my aunt
Annie appeared, telling me my dead mother
was in the arms of Jesus.
And, I kid you not, for a moment
I rose straight into the sky, felt a weird
exultation at the prospect of joining my mom
in Heaven someday. All my questions
about God and faith had been answered, a door
slammed shut on my persistent doubt.

How can I describe the *feeling* of being swept into the sky?
My therapist told me it was just a subconscious salve
for all my hopes and worries, how it was no more real
than the fabric of sleep itself, which I imagined
as a thin cotton shirt flapping on a line
sometime in 1965, back when my mom
was young and black bangs down hung over her forehead.

So, was I saved in my dream? Is this the way Jesus reaches
us as we wander through this vale of toil and sin?
Do we find real answers in sleep? Just ask

the Asmat, headhunters in coastal New Guinea,
who believed there was no difference between sleep and day
light, that dreams were as real as the giant crocodiles they hunted
for much-needed protein. Sometimes they ate the small birds
that sang from the depths of the mangroves, and sometimes
they ate insects, and yes, sometimes
they ate each other, assumed the life of the one
who was eaten, dreamed the world through the dead
man's sleep, followed his life story through rainy
afternoons when they were embraced

by old spirits summoned from Bisj poles,
altars carved faithfully from a single nutmeg branch.

When I was a little Baptist boy, I faithfully went
to St. Mark's Methodist on Sunday mornings
and waited for the Savior's embrace, looked
forward to the moment I walked from the pew
to the altar, where the preacher
would affirm my salvation as my grandma
and mother cried, as the entire
congregation sang me into Paradise.
I'm still waiting, trembling with doubt
in old age as one by one the Baptists
are whisked away in black Chevrolets
dressed in their Sunday best, wearing
lilac powder and cheap perfumes. This bright Florida

morning I still hear the faithful
singing, and in old age, I love them more, love
the way they trusted the life of the spirit, the way
they honored words passed down for two thousand
years, and were able to make the leap from syllable
to belief, from fragile human to eternal soul.

I am left here with dreams and doubt, with a longing
that cannot be defined in language, with a sorrow
that rises up from deep in my bones and speaks
of a place where all the rivers are dry beds of rock
and ghosts, where the mountains rise in the distance
like blue meanings stitched across a black night.

Jenny Bates

Inimitable Losses

the desire of the moth for the star - Percy Bysshe Shelley

Vultures glide effortless through bare branches. Seamed and seamless
as Jackson Pollock painting.

My pup tries to catch rivulets flowing in thin streams, sediments
washed away.

It all started with not pushing in a chair when
finished with it.

Sidewalk trees, lonely for neat cement paths around their trunks,
trodden by nimble feet.

I prefer to cut through the wild uncertain
alley.

Community sluggard, passive to neighborhood schools,
parks, play.

Tramps torment sinister poverty, the coward
rich.

Human sediment whose home never moves, meaning nothing.
Mud eaten as a delicacy.

What picture do I paint? for my pup as we stand under bright Benetnash
—

the principle mourner — Coyotes sing, I'd rather be with them.

Emily Jon Tobias

Red Cardboard Hearts Hanging From Strings

He'd been clear with you early on that having a family was never part of his game plan. You'd assumed he'd change his mind when he married you in a King County courthouse on a stormy Thursday in February. You wore a black dress, forgetting about the holiday altogether. No bouquet, no corsage, not even a rose tucked behind your ear. Why? *Because I'm allergic, Liza, fuck. How many times do I have to say it?*

A court reporter dressed in pink filed her nails. She batted eyelashes at the oversized bailiff as he ducked under red cardboard hearts hanging from strings. The whole damn thing was late getting started which forced the vows to be read like the end of some commercial for prescription drugs. You could've taken this as a sign. But when the judge pronounced you man and wife, there you stood, secretly wishing he'd eventually cave and want to raise some kids. He never did.

Tuesday in November. You first saw him at a trendy spot on Queen Anne where *Cocktails and Conversation* was posted across an A-frame sidewalk sign. Rain-smudged chalk made the fancy name for happy hour questionable. Yes, there were cocktails, but the conversation bit was falsely advertised. Your two remaining girlfriends ordered a cocktail each and closed out their tabs.

There's a cute guy over there, you'd said, pointing him out with a subtle nod.

Come on, Liza, who are you kidding? Sonia said.

What's that supposed to mean? you asked.

Tash rolled her eyes. Your life would get a lot less reckless if you just came out of that fucking closet you're in, she said.

With mouths to feed, your two remaining girlfriends went home before the hour was up. Lingering at the bar, you spotted him again resting on an elbow with cuffs undone and sleeves rolled, leaning into his hip, like some Law and Order detective. He loosened his tie and unbuttoned his collar, shoving the tiny straw to the side of his glass to take a full drink from the rim. He sucked on an ice cube, then bit down.

There was no first date. In fact, you skipped the whole dating phase altogether. After the second night out, you awoke in his bed the next morning with your tongue like a cat's. Whisky fumes seeped through your skin as you cupped a hand over your mouth to get a whiff. Shower running. Was he in it? You lifted the silk sheet to determine how far the night had gone. Bra, intact and clasped, one breast spilling out the right cup. When you touched along your hipline, an image of your Jewish mother sprang up like a jack-in-the-box at the absence of your underwear. *Fuck.* Pillow clasped to your front, you kicked your feet wild, as if drowning. Finally, there it was, your thong, stuck like a dryer sheet in a ball at the bottom of the bed. Hooked by your big toe, you slipped it on before the water turned off, as if he'd be shocked to find you indecent.

Dizzy holiday months went on like this, your hangovers like skid marks on an otherwise romantic Sunday drive. Your two remaining girlfriends stopped calling, making things much easier on you. You'd grown weary of pretending. In the early days, you'd walk him to his office on 3rd Avenue in the mornings; you, head pounding, still slick with sleep and sex, him, clean-shaven, smelling of musk, just to kiss him out from under the umbrella and wait to see him again. Then, you'd stop home during the day to feed your cat, conversing with the feline about how well you thought things were going with the man.

On one of these mornings, he'd said, I will take care of you forever, slipping a black AMEX from his hand to yours like passing a love note.

Eventually, you'd forgotten to feed your cat for almost a week. No matter, as it turns out, the man is allergic to just about everything, requiring you to abandon the animal at the humane society before he'd allow you to move things into his cushy loft in West Seattle facing the city skyline. Small price to pay for a view like that, you'd thought.

Shortly after the move-in, on a romantic Thursday night in, you seared steaks as advised by the Food Network you'd watched all day waiting for him to return from work. This is perfectly cooked, he'd said. You've done so well, you deserve a little fun tonight. He held up a small baggie, swaying it back and forth. After the first line, he ran his hand along your thigh (you suddenly smelled the peppermint of Helena's skin). He clinked his glass of expensive red wine against yours over and over (while the memory of the edges of her face blurred...but damn, that fine golden fuzz rising along her cheekbones where you touched her...more wine, more powder, more, more, more...erased).

Eventually, a long night of brainstorming ensued, as if one of his corporate deadlines loomed, and the creative idea of marriage turned on like a light bulb. Einstein would've been proud of how your heads came together. An impulsive agreement to marry led to frantic celebratory fucking during which neither of you finished. Sleepless at dawn, the sunrise quivered like a frying egg behind Pier 66. A bright sun broken like a yolk. Your runny emotions (regret) oozed all over his frustrated face. Clouds cracked like little shells in the pan while you both hid your eyes.

A crumpled $20 lay on the table after he rushed out late for the office the next day. No AMEX card. You called in sick to your waitressing gig one time too many the following night, still nursing your hangover with the hair of the dog during the day. He squeezed his husky arms around you when you told him how sorry you were that you'd made him late. How sorry you were that you'd been canned. How sorry you were that you hadn't been pulling your weight. That you'd try to find another job just as quickly as possible.

There, there, he'd said, I'm sure you'll make it up to me somehow.

You've been unemployed ever since.

*

Monday (the day you'd finally leave him), 8:30 a.m. (although you don't know it, yet).

I will meet you at Benihana's tonight at 7:30, Liza. Don't be late, he warns you, stuffing papers into his briefcase.

How could I be late to our fifth anniversary dinner? Have some faith in your wife, you say. You still love how saying *wife* sounds off your tongue, despite the circumstances.

I mean it, Liza. Do not be late. Gotta be on my game. The boss flies in for that big client meeting early tomorrow. *Remember?* It's crunch time, Liza. Make it or break it. Not that you'd know anything about that. He rolls his eyes. God damn it, this fucking rash is driving me nuts, he says, one hand down his pants, the other stuffing a muffin in his mouth.

The last time he'd taken you to Benihana's was soon after tying the knot. An exotic night out, to celebrate and watch the knives fly, he'd said. There was no honeymoon. In fact, you skipped the whole honeymoon phase altogether. Real life resumed.

Shortly thereafter, right around the time you lost the baby, he began beating you above the neck in places you couldn't cover. You weren't surprised by the pregnancy, given that you'd stopped taking your birth control pills without his permission. You were, however, shocked by the first slap to the face given that you'd never had the courage to tell him you'd conceived.

He downs the last sip of coffee. I'm late, he says. I'll see you tonight. Be good. He swoops his BMW keys off the counter. Under the keys, he's left you a to-do list with a $50 covering the Post-it. #1) Get itch cream from Rite-Aid. #2) Laundry. We're out of detergent. #3) DO NOT BE LATE FOR DINNER! You stick the bill in the waistline of your yoga pants, yanking off the plastic nub of a Marshall's tag. You kick off the new running shoes he bought you for your anniversary and slump into his leather recliner.

Five years? Five *fucking* years. You pinch your arm near the bicep, flexing your muscle. The skin crinkles like tissue paper. You pull the meat from the bone, poke at an orangish bruise.

Remote? Tucked down the crack of the chair from when he fell asleep the night before, snoring by the second half of the Seahawks game. Television, on. Good Morning America and sweet Michael Strahan. God, he's delicious (for a man).

You think back to the signs. Like those bruises in fingerprints on upper arms that time you were in his beloved La-Z-Boy (yes, ironic) when the game started...that welt from a playful snap to the bra when you took his fat joke too seriously...the handprint that lingered on your ass for days past rough sex on a tipsy (blacked out) Saturday afternoon. You hate yourself for missing the obvious. Any halfwit would've seen the signs. You never did.

Michael introduces the guest, some sleek L.A. fitness guru / food expert / empathic life-coach. Perfect hair, this one. Like she's just stepped off the beach, you can smell the sun on her skin through the screen. And she's not afraid to go au naturale in the face either, just some simple foundation, no lipstick, just gloss. Sliding from the chair onto hands and knees, you lean in close to the HD TV. Not a wrinkle to be found. You yank back on the skin of your face along the jawline as if she's looking back at you. Staring at the screen, it's as you're moving face-first through a windstorm.

GMA's guru has light hair that bounces when she turns her head, then sweeps perfectly along her bare shoulders coming to stillness before she opens her mouth. Uncanny likeness to... hard to name her, even now. (Helena Rose Halprin, after her grandmother.)

Hello friends. Today I'm going to tell you some of my secrets to living your best life, the guru says, as *Simple Solutions for Expanding Your Horizons* flashes across the screen in bold letters. The expert rolls out her first secret to life: #1) *Go out and get spiritual!*

The woman giggles then, that L.A. kind of laugh, perfectly constrained. What about your meager attempt at a religious resurgence when you volunteered at the local Jewish Community Center in the daycare room? This you found to be somehow comforting, being safe amongst your former people, until you arrived one day still reeking of cigarettes and booze from the night before. You were promptly released from duty, but only after you heard the secretary telling her rabbi, Smoking is for trashy *goyim*! and how she would have none of your kind in a room alone with their children. If she only knew, you'd thought. *L'chaim*.

You knew you were doomed as a Jew at age sixteen. Coming

home on the last sundown of Hanukkah with your first tattoo. *Barukh ata adonai*, you sing and light the match…*Eloheinu melekh ha'olam*…the candle wobbles…you reach to catch the menorah from falling, your sleeve inching up. Your mother sees the small heart tattooed on your inner wrist.

Liza, what have you done! She spits when she shouts. I've had it with you! Did you even think about your great-grandmother in the camps? They carved a number on her arm, Liza. And so many others. Did you think about *that*?

You'd only seen your mother cry twice before. And now even in death, she goes on, you'll be separate from us. You can't be buried in the family cemetery with that disgraceful thing on your arm. She leaves you standing there with wax dripping down your hand.

You couldn't really blame her for thinking you were a bad seed. The day before that, your mother had come home early from work unexpectedly. And there you were, smoking a cigarette under the garage overhang in a rainstorm (thanking god it wasn't her she'd found you with), while Bill Braxton waited pantsless and shivering inside the house after he'd taken your virginity, his erection most likely shriveled to pea size. The tattoos were meant to memorialize your blossoming love.

It never did. For you, the tattoo was revenge.

Later that school year, Bill moved on to some cheerleader named (gorgeous) Gretchen. You'd taken a cab to the clinic, alone, to terminate the pregnancy. Given that you were already tattooed and banished, you're never quite sure why you couldn't just come clean and tell your mother. Maybe, you'd thought, there was still time to redeem yourself. You never did.

Now, in the kitchen with a view of the screen, you pour yourself chardonnay and a splash of OJ over a few ice cubes. The first sip smooths the space between your eyebrows. You run a sponge across the counter and wash his dirty coffee mug by hand.

You dry your hands, tuning into the next two expert suggestions from Ms. L.A.

#2) *Make a commitment to prepare your own food.* Cooking classes, Williams Sonoma. You quit after he spat out your first attempt at eggs benedict unsupervised.

#3) *Practice seeing the world with new eyes.* Epic failure photography class he paid for at the community college. You dropped out after he found the charge for your new camera on his credit card bill (*What the fuck Liza? $1500 for a fucking camera? Who do you think you are, Ansel fucking Adams?*).

Finishing your drink, you peel a banana and stuff half the thing down your throat. Then, you pour another, this time in a sport top water bottle. You clip a jogger fanny pack around your waist, slipping the bottle into its holder.

*

At noon, a reminder alerts you to call his office for the required midday check-in.

Hey baby. How's your day going? you ask.

You've been drinking, Liza. I can hear it in your voice, he says.

You turn up the volume on the television, open the sport top with your teeth and squeeze. I am not, you say. I'm cleaning the house. You slip the bottle back into its holster like a weapon.

Liza, I am not stupid. Do you think I'm some kind of idiot? I know what you're up to. You'd think for just one day you could keep your shit in check. My whole fucking year of work is on the line tomorrow. I don't need to be stressing about you. Not today.

Come on. Don't start now. It's our anniversary. We're supposed to celebrate, you say.

If you're not at the fucking restaurant at 7:30 in an Uber, you're fucked, Liza. If you are there, we'll celebrate. Be good, he says, and hangs up.

With your left thumb, you spin the wedding band around your finger. You hike your yoga pants and tighten the fanny pack. Until tomorrow, Michael Strahan. You blow him a kiss and grab the remote, stabbing at the power button.

With a laundry basket tucked under one arm, you gather Calvin Klein boxers off the bathroom floor, using his favorite pair as a rag to catch a spider that's nested in the corner. You run his underwear along the floor board, then wring them out in the toilet. You open the vanity drawer to find your script of Valium. One left. Next to that, your birth control. You pop Monday's into your palm and swallow both pills with a squirt of chard.

Moving to the bedroom, you scoop up dirty dress socks scattered under the bed, on the dresser, billowing out from the hamper in the closet. You slide into a pair of his socks to sweep the floor with your feet as you go. You strip the bed of silk sheets, running your foot under the bed. Something bounces off your toe and slides across the hardwoods coming out the other side. A cell phone.

His phone? No, you'd called him on his phone, right? You sit on the naked mattress, touch the phone to turn it on. Internet browser history. *U-District Super Hot Blonde Waiting For You....A Touch of Heaven $99 Asian Special...No Expectations - Sexy Freaky Older Cougar Just Looking for a Good Time...* Then, photos from three years back. Is that you? Naked on this very bed, passed out, face up, legs and arms sprawled. With shaking hands, you scroll. Who's this now? Is it...no, is it you again? That's your hair on the head pushed between his legs. That's your behind arched up in the air. That's your mouth wrapped around him. Zoom in. A small red heart tattooed on the inner wrist of the hand he pins to the bed. He'd always said that Jewish girls give the best head. You'd tried to like it, for him. You never did.

You drop the phone. Carefully slide it back under the bed with your foot. In your nightstand drawer, you find the prescription you'd tried so hard not to fill. Slipping it in your fanny pack, you rip his dirty socks off your feet. You pop the lid on the washing machine, dumping in the load. No detergent. Post-it, right. *Fuck.* $50, enough? You'll run (walk) to the drug store. You can do this.

*

On the walk back home, you decide it's over. Bag in hand, outside Rite-Aid, you watch a bird perched on a blue reserved parking space sign. The crow squawks, then craps on the head of a stick figure in a wheelchair. You've seen the sign, and in this case, bird shit will do.

You walk slowly, hair pulled back into a low tight ponytail, fanny pack bouncing off your hip. You take your time. In one hand, a bag filled with your prescription, a bottle of Smirnoff, and extra-strength scented Tide, with Febreze even, abundantly allergenic. You'd asked the pharmacist where to find the itch cream just so you could have a stare-off with the tube, as if you were winning against him when you decided not to buy it.

The plastic bag swings at your side as you walk. With your free hand, you drink. Heavy rains have brought lush down on the rolling summer-brown hills behind the Sound. In the distance, three stark white crosses are staked, exaggerated, as if in bold print, saying to you, Come this way. You never did. Instead, you keep walking. Where Harbor Avenue crosses under the bridge, a homeless woman sells roses out of a bucket. You buy two dozen with the remainder of his money.

Back at the loft, it's well past 5:00 when you smell the Tide and smile, adding two capfuls to the washing machine already loaded with his dirty boxers and socks and silk bed sheets. When the dryer buzzer sounds, you fold each of his items perfectly before setting them in his drawer. Then, you prepare the bed. You stretch the fitted sheet diagonally, corner to corner. Shaking the top sheet free of lint first, you let it balloon naturally around the mattress. Smoothing across the top, you tuck the sheet under the mattress into neatly folded crisp hospital corners, just as your mother had taught you. There, you say to yourself, perfect.

Next, you vase one of the rose bunches, fanning them into an arrangement on the kitchen counter. You set the vase aside a Post-It on which you've written, Happy Fucking Anniversary, with three little hearts dotting the end. With the other dozen, you rip petals off, walking backwards toward the bedroom, leaving a trail to the bed. You've taken a paring knife with you, late-night-ordered off the Home Shopping Network, along with the remaining items from Rite-Aid. With the knife you carefully dethorn each stem, leaving barbed bits floating to the floor with the petals.

You reach under the bed for the cell phone and rest it next to you sitting on the bed. Ahead you see the trail of thorns and petals you've left with a view of the fragrant red roses like a sign to stop. You unroll the paper pharmacy bag and twist off the Smirnoff cap, setting the open bottle on the floor in front of you. Then, you pry the cap off the pills and empty the bottle into your hand.

Steady now, steady. Pills on wet palm, face up, set on your thigh. Other hand on knife to your side. Close your eyes. Breathe. You can do this. Right, yes, you will, you *will* do this. But then, then, wait.

Wait because you smell her everywhere- the one, you put your clumsy mouth against in a closet in 5th grade - the one, who always sang Led Zeppelin songs off-key, low, at midnight, high and under the stars - the one, you loved all the way up to Bill Braxton when you moved onto boys but only because she did - the one. The one you thought you'd forget. You never did.

You look down. Flat palm, pills, inner wrist, bulging vein. Stop. The heart.

You clamp your fist around the pills.

You lie back. And now, now, a vision of you and her, in a car filled with cherry blossoms. She drives ahead, you glance behind. A baby seat, strapped in, empty. In the rearview window, a sign says *Baby On Board*. You bring your hand softly to your belly.

Release the knife. Sit up, you. Straighten.

You do.

Salt from a fresh tear spreads dark like blood would, on the pillow where your head was. You grab his phone, spilling the pills on the carpet at your feet. Quickly, you scroll, swiping through those photos of you as if you're on a train, speeding by. Come on, come on...there. A video. The only one.

Who's that? You've met her. *Her?* It can't be, can it? It is. His boss's wife. You know for sure when you hear the high pitch tail end of a moan like that laugh of hers, after a few glasses of wine, at the holiday party, last year, when you swore you'd seen her wink.

Ahead of you, red roses in the kitchen flash like a railroad crossing. The train stops. You stall. Then, you remember. What he'd said when you'd asked him about that woman the day after the party, *You're fucking paranoid, Liza, and you were wasted. What the fuck do you know?*

You forward the video twice: once, to your phone; next, to the number in his contacts labeled Big Boss Man. Slowly then, with grace, you fluff his pillow, placing the knife delicately in the center, where his head goes. You smooth the bed covers and cap the Smirnoff, gathering as many pills as you can find to store back in the bottle. Then, you dig for that old Canon he bought on the top shelf of your closet. A final touch, you snap a photo of the whole scene, a real framer. To remember exactly what the last he'll see of you looks like.

Pulling the strap tight, you clip the fanny pack in place, sliding your pills into the main compartment. With one hand around the bottle and his phone in the other, you follow the trail of petals back to the kitchen, careful to avoid thorns. Your camera hangs around your neck. On the Post-It, at the very bottom, underneath the three hearts, you add, Don't forget your phone for your big meeting tomorrow. Good luck! Be good.

On the counter, you spin his phone like a top. As you're watching it slow and settle you uncap the Smirnoff. And drink.

For a moment, in the open air outside the front door, you wonder if your mother's banishment would have held true. Then you wonder what kind of cocktail he's ordered, while he waits for you.

Joan Barasovska

Drenched

There's no in-between for a person like me,
only up or down, drowning or sitting pretty
in the lifeguard's chair, tooting my whistle,
declaiming and super-brave.

There's the Diving Tank or the Kiddie Pool,
no Adult Swim. No designated lanes.
Admire me in my bikini on the high dive,
blindfolded and in love at the same time.

If I cry underwater, who would know?
Anyone can see I'm hardly swimming,
only the backstroke very, very slowly.
My fans stand by with a life preserver.

I was born without a snorkel or a skin.
No dry land, no lessons, just jump in.

John Haugh

Hatchet Lesson

When I was ten,
Dad taught me
to turn our pet
rabbits into meat
with a hatchet,
one fierce crunch
to kill with less pain,
then string her carcass
up in that obscene Y
before skinning
soul-soft fur like
peeling off a wet
leather glove.

Donna Love Wallace

Vulture

The foul, the fetid, the rotting putrid
fumes I smell, and turn. The best is a rune
spoken for the fresh dead. I want to breathe
its last breath, still hovering
over raw exposure, feel heat shimmer,
rise to my reddening cheek, dance
to the crisp, blackening singe of song.
Read the unread, unfledged, still being fed—
until it has grown to rise on its own, out-bound,
lay itself down again and again on
pages, pages, pages, landing in the hands
of bone marrow suckers hungry to muscle
into its deepest space, suckle the first blood made.

Cathy Adams

Wonders Without Number

Chapter 1

Summer, 1975

Every first Sunday of the month after church, Margie and her two children went to visit the midget. This was just the way Margie put it. She never said, "Let's go visit your cousin, Leonard." She just called him the midget. As soon as they escaped the morning service of Mount Corinth Bethel Baptist church, Kevin and his sister Dorothy opened the creaking doors of the green Thunderbird, hopped in, and Margie drove them from Valdosta to Kennebotton, Georgia. They went as much to see Sidwa, Margie's sister, as to see Leonard; still Margie referred to it as going to see the midget.

Margie lit up a Pall Mall as she accelerated the Thunderbird onto the freeway entrance ramp. While she talked her cigarette dangled between Aloha Pink painted nails and showered the front floorboard with ashes. "Now don't bring up anything about ya'll going swimming at the YMCA next weekend."

"Why not?" asked Kevin.

"Because then he'd want to go."

Kevin twisted a quarter-sized slice of peeling off the top of an orange and flicked it out the window. "So? Is there some kind of rule about that?"

Twisting her head around, she spat out her words. "You know what would happen! There are picnic tables in front of the concession stand and people are trying to *eat*. What would happen if we brought a little crippled midget in there? They'd practically be jumping out of the pool trying to stare at him," said Margie.

"Yeah, it's a good thing he's not black," said Kevin, just loud enough to hear.

"You shut your goddamn smart mouth right this minute!" Margie snapped her head around giving him the best I'm-gonna-slap-the-shit-out-of-you look a mother could muster.

Dorothy sat in the back with her bible in her lap praying aloud for Jesus to forgive her mother, ". . .and help us to walk closer to you, oh Lord Jesus. Amen."

"Are you finished now, Dorothy?"

"Yes ma'am."

"Good. Amen." Having a pious child annoyed Margie, but she retained just enough residual Baptist fear from her upbringing to stand clear of Dorothy's exercise of her beliefs. She really wanted to tell her to shut her goddamn mouth sometimes too, but she reserved that comment only for Kevin. Margie likened it to having a witch for a daughter; someone you never wanted to piss off because deep in Margie's heart she feared that someday God would strike her down right through Dorothy's Revelation eyes.

Margie had forbidden her from reading bible passages out loud in the car, so Dorothy was limited to reading pertinent scripture to her Aunt Sidwa who loved to tell how God tested her everyday by giving her a handicapped midget for a son. Except she didn't call him a midget either. No one did except Margie, at least not to his face. Everyone in the family had their names for Leonard. Granny Roland called him, "that little Leonard." His mother called him, "my dear sweet blessing," among other things. Dorothy called him "God's Special Gift." Kevin called him, "Leonard," a thought that seemed to escape the rest.

The drive to Leonard's house took an hour and fifteen minutes. For each visit they packed coconut macaroons, marshmallows, and Rice Krispie treats, Leonard's favorites. Margie usually made everything the night before, but last night she'd fallen asleep on the sofa watching a Charles Bronson movie marathon. This morning she was up at 7:00 AM stirring marshmallows and butter in a saucepan while listening to Wilson Pickett on WDUG.

It was busting 90, as Margie liked to put it, when they pulled the Thunderbird next to the overgrown crepe myrtle in Leonard and Sidwa's yard. The white wood house was so entrenched amongst the dogwoods, juniper bushes, nandinias, and pine trees, it seemed to have roots of its own, and to somehow pluck it out would have damaged the ecosystem. Somewhere deep under the house the myriad network of roots must be intertwined.

In her yard, Sidwa collected gnomes, trolls, deer, garden maidens, rabbits, dancing bears, and even a cement reproduction of the Statue of Liberty which she draped in an American flag each July 4th. Stationed to the far side of the crepe myrtle, the flamingos wore tiny seasonal hats Sidwa made herself. She had parked Leonard's tiny white wooden chair next to her own in front of the girl flamingo that wore a white bonnet trimmed in plastic cherries. Leonard's forearm crutches were leaned against his lower legs which dangled in front of the chair. The chair was a yard sale purchase, once a part of a doll's tea table set. In his green, wide brimmed garden hat and poly-cotton yellow trousers that Granny Roland had made for him, he looked like a carnival prize. Granny Roland, who was actually no one's grandmother, was always making him clothes from leftover fabric. Leonard owned a shirt, vest, or pair of pants resembling every baby blanket, tablecloth or pair of curtains Granny Roland had ever stitched.

"How's the-- how ya'll doing?" Margie shouted, pushing the car door shut with a kick. She carried the tray of Rice Krispie treats in one hand and a paper sack with coconut macaroons and marshmallows in her other.

"Look Sweet Blessing, Aunt Margie's brought you some more treats." Sidwa placed her bowl of snap beans on the grass beside her and stood up. Leonard remained eerily still in his chair. His head lolled back and his hands lay lifeless on the armrests. A fly lit just under his left eye and he fought the urge to swat it away, his only movement being two nearly imperceptible twitches. The fly departed his cheek bone, circled his face, and landed on his chin.

Kevin let his door fall shut behind him and sighed hard in the stagnant heat. Trying to remain as inconspicuous as possible, he peered around the front windshield at his cousin. For a second

Leonard blended in perfectly with a family of gnomes to the right of the flamingoes. Next to Leonard's chair, a red-hatted gnome held a basket of something that must have once been daisies, except now the petals spilling over the ceramic edges were mottled brown from dead foliage that settled on it year after year. The gnome grinned over a basket of what looked like tobacco spit. Kevin's mother stopped in front of Leonard and dipped her head down, staring at him. "Is he sick?"

"He's playing the game again. Ignore it. You know it never lasts long once Kevin and Dorothy are here." Sidwa's face opened in a wide grin at Dorothy who remained stupefied at the sight of Leonard, deep in his game.

"Dorothy, that is the prettiest little dress," said Sidwa. "I swear you are cuter than the Sunbeam Bread girl."

"Thank you, Aunt Sidwa," Dorothy gushed.

Kevin hovered beside the car, trying to balance on one foot with his hands behind his back. Margie motioned him over. "Here, take this in the kitchen. When Leonard's done with his," she waved a hand toward his lifeless body, "whatever it is he's doing, he'll be hungry." Kevin took the tray and the sack from his mother and disappeared through the front door, letting the screen slam shut behind him.

Leonard was fourteen years old, but he could have passed for six, or twenty. It was hard to tell. "Leonard, sweetie, we've talked about this. You promised."

"I can say a prayer for him," Dorothy offered, her voice not much more than a whisper.

"I've said so many prayers over this dear sweet child heaven is probably tired of listening to me," said Sidwa.

"Oh, no ma'am. Heaven never gets tired of prayers," said Dorothy.

Margie pulled one of Sidwa's lawn chairs next to Leonard's seat, placing him between the two of them. Sidwa took her seat again.

"So, you said on the phone you met somebody. You gonna tell me about him?" said Margie, her eyes open as wide as the July sunlight would allow. Turning to retrieve her bowl of snap beans, Sidwa maneuvered her lips in a wordless response.

"What's that supposed to mean?" said Margie.

"I'm not saying there's anything to it."

"It doesn't sound like you're saying anything at all about it so far," said Margie. "Now my little sister doesn't call me at 10:30 at night just to chat about nothing then ends the call with 'Oh, and I met the sweetest man. I'll tell you all about it when you get here on Sunday.'"

The kitchen door smacked shut again and Kevin stepped onto the cement porch. When he put a hand on his hip and stood with his feet apart and his head tilted back, he exuded the same defiant expression his mother was so good at. He held his position in the center of the porch, spying the inert Leonard with squinted eyes.

"Honey, why don't you go sit on the porch swing with your brother?" said Margie to her daughter. Dorothy stumbled forward before darting off to the porch. Sidwa took it for an awkward curtsey and giggled.

"That child is an angel," said Sidwa.

"An angel of the apocalypse," Margie muttered half to herself.

"He's a furniture salesman," said Sidwa.

"A what?"

"The man I told you about. He's an industrial furniture salesman."

"What the heck is industrial furniture?"

Sidwa flicked the rotten end of a snap bean onto the ground and sighed hard. "Well it's, I don't know. Big sofas and chairs like you sit in when you're in a waiting area of some place."

"How did you meet him?"

"In the dentist's office. Leonard was having a check-up and we met in Dr. Knetton's waiting room."

"He doesn't have any teeth," said Leonard. It took a second for Margie to register that he had spoken.

"What? Who doesn't have any teeth? Your dentist?" asked Margie.

"Mr. Billings doesn't have any teeth. He wears dentures. He can click them with his tongue and make them jump, like this," said Leonard. Leonard flicked his tongue at the top of his mouth and made a sound like a June bug jumping across a garbage can lid.

"Leonard, what a rude thing to say," said Sidwa. "Mr. Billings is a very nice man. He gave you that little toy set of office furniture to play with."

Leonard turned his face to his mother and continued clicking his tongue.

"It's cute as can be. It's a little red plastic desk, a sofa, and a stuffed chair that he uses for models when he's showing samples to businesses," said Sidwa.

"Maybe you can use it to pretend you're a CEO," suggested Margie, refusing to look at Leonard on account of his drooling face.

Leonard pulled the front of his shirt tail from his pants and wiped it across his mouth. "What's a See-E-Oh?"

"It's a Chief Executer Officer, something like that. It's head of a company."

"Aren't you a See-E-Oh?" asked Leonard.

"I reckon running your own hair salon in your home could make you a CEO. Yeah, I'm a CEO if there ever was one."

"I'm glad you brought that up, because I want you to color my hair. It's on the kitchen cabinet whenever you're ready."

"Why do you need me to help you color your hair? Any idiot can follow the directions on those boxes."

"You remember what happened last time."

"You can't buy something called Sassy 'N Classy and then get mad when your hair turns out looking like some south Georgia stripper's," she said.

Leonard started laughing, first slow and low, then it escalated into a rapid *eh-heh-heh-heh* until Sidwa's mouth turned into a hard white line. "Honey, go on up and see your cousins." On the porch Kevin was hitting the porch floor with his feet on every back swing causing the seat to jerk before each forward thrust. Dorothy held onto her bible with her right hand and clenched the chain that secured the arm of the swing with her left.

"Aw Mama," Leonard said.

"Be a good host, now," said Sidwa. "They brought you Rice Krispie snacks. Your Aunt Margie goes to a lot of trouble to fix those." She raised her eyebrows one time and nodded her head toward the bored children on the porch.

Leonard's face turned up in a smile like a television game show host. "Thank you Aunt Margie for the delicious snacks." He placed his pudgy hand on her shoulder and patted her lightly before sliding his arms into his crutches. Keeping his smile aimed at Margie's face, he stepped a half circle around her before turning his body toward the children and walking away. His torso swung severely from left to right as he made his way to the porch.

"He's walking real good now," said Margie.

"I just hope nothing happens to him."

"Like what? He looks fine to me." The two sisters watched Leonard walk away in silence. Leonard was born an achondroplastic dwarf, and he learned to love the sound of the words as if it meant he belonged to an elite tribe of primitive people. Whenever someone in a grocery store or the bakery or the courthouse made some comment about his diminutive size, he pointed out his medical condition. If the perpetrator were a child and his mother was not directly within earshot, Leonard would whisper that he got that way from drinking too much milk as a baby, or wearing his shoes too tight, or eating a toad. Sometimes when children ran away shrieking, Sidwa would eye Leonard suspiciously as he smiled his sunbeam smile at her. When they were out in public she was almost always close enough to hear his whispers, and Leonard was left with little recourse other than turning his back on her and picking his nose or turning his eyelids inside out until the child's revulsion of Leonard's behavior outweighed his fascination with Leonard's body.

Leonard ascended the four steps of the porch one at a time, lifting each leg deliberately as he swung his body left, right, left, right, until he was on the porch. Kevin stopped the swing and waited to see if Leonard wanted to climb on. Leonard cocked his head up high and said, "Hey, remember that time we were wrestling on the porch?"

Kevin scratched at the corner of his mouth and looked out into the yard. "I remember. You acted like you had rabies or something, biting my leg so hard I had a blood blister. And who did your mama blame it on? Me."

"That was fun."

"I nearly got my ass busted."

"I almost had you," said Leonard. He stood in front of Kevin with his hands on his hips, grinning in a way that felt like a dare to Kevin, though he couldn't say why.

"Had me, my eye. I had both your hands around your back," said Kevin, resuming his swinging.

"Did I tell you about going to the wrestling match at the VFW?"

"When?"

"Mama took me about two weeks ago. The Muckraker and Trucking Tony Trinidad were fighting. Guess who they called up to the ring for the warm-up?"

Dorothy's eyes grew large and she dipped her head forward. "Did you get to wrestle in a real wrestling match?"

"It's just this warm-up thing they do. They let somebody from the audience come up before the real match begins and try to wrestle with the champion. It's usually some kid." Leonard waited to see if Kevin would take the bait. "Don't you want to hear what happened?"

"What happened?" asked Kevin.

"I got the Muckraker in a headlock. I guess he wasn't expecting it. He was just horsing around, thinking I didn't know how to do anything like that. I caught him by the throat like this." Leaning on one crutch, he made a sideways circle with his arms and curled his fingers around an imaginary neck. "He was so surprised he didn't even move for a few seconds."

"A headlock, huh?" said Kevin.

"Yeah, but I let him go real quick. It was just horsing around, you know."

"So, how'd you reach his neck?" asked Kevin.

"He got down on his knees, so it'd be fair."

"Lucky you," said Kevin.

"It's no lie. You can ask Mama. She saw the whole thing." Leonard pointed back at his mother.

Kevin stopped the swing a moment. "So, you got your hands all the way around the Muckraker's head and locked your fingers together like so. That right?"

"Yeah, if you don't believe me come on down here and I'll show you just how I did it," said Leonard.

"Kevin, Mama'll kill you if you go fighting with Leonard again," said Dorothy.

"And his head is about as big as a garbage can," Kevin continued, ignoring Dorothy. "I'll give you a dollar if you can get *me* in a headlock. Let alone the Muckraker." Leonard removed his straw hat, tossed it onto the swing, and lay his crutches down on either side, precariously planting his unsteady feet a few additional inches apart.

"Wait a minute, let me empty my pockets." Kevin pulled out a yo-yo, a miniature yellow Trans-Am, two nickels, and a rabbit's foot. "All right, I'm ready," he said taking two steps until he was only a few inches from Leonard's crouching body.

Leonard stole a glance over his shoulder at his mother whose face was completely blocked by Margie's as they discussed Sidwa's furniture salesman. Leonard was 3' 1" tall. His legs bowed out like an infant's, and his arms curved slightly making him look like a walking stuffed bear. His chest was slightly barrel shaped, giving the appearance of being perpetually on the verge of exhaling deeply. In his yellow pants he looked as if he were held up by two enormous bananas. Kevin almost laughed out loud at the sight and it was at that moment that Leonard lunged for Kevin's knees, toppling him to the porch floor in an instant. Kevin was so taken by surprise that he lay there kicking his feet, until Leonard maneuvered his arms up and wrapped them around Kevin's neck, attempting to get the fingers of his left hand locked around the fingers of his right. Kevin managed to roll Leonard on his side, kicking and pushing furiously at his cousin, but Leonard held tight like a coil of copper threatening to pop loose.

"I got you!" Leonard hissed, his strength concentrated so intensely on Kevin that he could barely push the words out. They were drowned out momentarily by an emergency vehicle with its siren blaring. Its droning whine died in the distance as it raced past the house and down Shotsdale Road.

Kevin's words were muffled against his older cousin's short arms. "It don't count until you got your fingers together," Kevin said. He braced his curled toes against the cement floor of the porch and managed to flip the two of them over so that he was on top, but Leonard still held tightly to his neck from underneath.

"You little snot!" Kevin managed to shove an arm between his neck and Leonard who struggled underneath.

"Kevin! You stop that this minute before I whip the hell out of you!" Margie ran toward the porch with Sidwa a step behind her.

"Leonard! Kevin, get off of him or I'll get a hickory switch after you myself!" Sidwa pushed past her sister and leaped onto the porch in two steps. Leonard released Kevin immediately and the two of them rolled apart, breathless and glancing at one another to see who would make a defense. Leonard groped for his crutches and

Sidwa helped to pull him to his feet. She began running her hands over his back, arms, and shoulders like a blind person memorizing her son for all eternity. She kept asking, "Does this hurt?" Leonard shook his head to each question, all the while exchanging wordless, squint-eyed boy threats with Kevin. When Sidwa was satisfied he was still whole, she let her body droop and she took a deep breath. "You boys can not play like that. Do you know what it would do to Leonard to get a broken bone? Lord goodness, we have made so many trips to the orthopedic surgeon up in Albany."

"Do you see what you've done to your aunt? Can you see that?" Margie pointed at her sister and waited for a reply from Kevin.

Sidwa sat on her knees and resumed gripping Leonard all over. "My precious boy. My sugar pie."

"He was doing it, too," argued Kevin.

"He was doing it, too?" yelled Margie. "What if I was to go into Bargain Town and start shoplifting hot curlers and car wax and ironing boards, anything I liked? And when they asked me why I was doing it I pointed to somebody else and said, 'She was doing it, too.' What do you think they would say?"

Kevin remained on the porch floor aghast and bewildered at his mother's analogy. He flipped her words over in is mind, trying to make some logic of it, but finding none, he remained silent. Whenever he or his sister got into trouble with Leonard it was always found to be anyone's fault except Leonard's. Never had he wanted to smash his cousin's head between two bricks more than he did at that moment. Aunt Sidwa may as well put Leonard in a glass box and have him carried around like he was a boy made of tissue paper the way she carried on. Just going to Leonard's house meant a butt chewing for Kevin whether he started anything or not. He made up his mind right then to punch Leonard at the next available opportunity just to make it all worth the trouble.

Margie was not going to let the Walgreen story go. "Do you think I could get away with a defense like that? Huh? Do you?" She was ending her sentence with a "do you" which in Kevin's experience always meant he was to answer in the negative.

Cathy Adams **149**

"No, ma'am."

"Of course not. I swear I don't know what I'm going to do with you. And Dorothy, you just stood by and didn't call for help."

Dorothy's mouth quivered and her eyes watered. Everyone looked at one another for a moment before Margie, who had taken control of the situation by maternal default, started up again, waving her hands in frustration. "Ten minutes! We can't be here ten minutes without you kids getting into some kind of trouble."

Sidwa put a hand on Leonard's head and pulled him to her waist. "My dear sweet blessing," she murmured followed by a sigh. "I reckon we can do my hair now."

"If you think you can behave yourselves out here without breaking the front porch off the house," said Margie. "I guess ya'll can have those Rice Krispies now. Surely ya'll can sit here and eat without somebody getting a concussion!" She snatched the screen door open and went inside.

When the three children were chewing silently on the porch swing, Sidwa reluctantly left Leonard sitting between his cousins and followed Margie back into the house.

Kevin pushed the porch swing back and forth in silence, the three of them sitting arm to arm as they chewed on the Rice Krispies. It was nearly three o'clock in the afternoon and the dead air was like a dog's breath. Moving back and forth in the swing gave them the illusion of a breeze.

Dorothy wiped each corner of her mouth with her index finger. "We went to church camp this summer. Kevin saw a snake by the pond and it swam right out over the water with his head up like this." She stretched out her arm and tilted her hand up until it was vertical with the ground, zig-zagging it through the air in front of Leonard's face.

"Anybody get bit?" asked Leonard.

"No, of course not. It was church camp."

"So?" said Leonard. "Snakes don't know it's church camp. They might think it's just plain old Boy Scout camp and bite somebody anyway."

"Nobody got bit," said Kevin. "It was just a little water snake. Why do you have to go and try to make something out of nothing all the time?"

"We're only going to be here about another hour then Mama'll be ready to go home. Be nice to Leonard, okay?" Dorothy said.

"Why do you still have to use those funny looking crutches? You don't need them," said Kevin.

"Mama says my bones are weak on account of all the operations I've had. I reckon she'd have a duck if I didn't use them."

"Your step-dad used to say you could walk without them," said Kevin.

"He didn't know what he was talking about," said Leonard.

"I wish your stupid step-dad would come back so Mama wouldn't make us come over here to visit all the time," said Kevin. For once Leonard kept quiet. He held his half eaten Rice Krispie treat in his hand, the half-chewed bite suddenly dry as cardboard on his tongue. Kevin stopped eating a moment, too. His words made a hard thud inside his own stomach, and suddenly he knew they had hurt Leonard much more than the scuffle on the floor. He wanted to take it back out of the air, but he couldn't stand the thought of apologizing to Leonard.

"He didn't mean that," said Dorothy.

"He's dead now anyway," said Leonard.

"How do you know?" said Kevin.

Leonard's sneering face was only inches from Kevin's. "Because I just know it, that's why. That's why we haven't heard anything from him in two years."

"So why hasn't Aunt Sidwa told us that?"

"'Cause she don't know it like I know it, that's why," said Leonard.

"That doesn't make any sense," said Kevin, but his last words were drowned out by the fast approaching vehicle with the siren again. The white car was heading in the opposite direction as it had come before, but this time instead of rushing past, when it got nearly to Sidwa's driveway the driver screeched on the brakes and the car pulled in behind Margie's Thunderbird. Red letters on the side door read "Fire Department: Colquitt County." A tall man with an enormous chest and arms opened the driver's side and stepped out. Another man, much thinner and smaller than the first, got out from the passenger's side. He held a map in front of him and kept shaking his head and sighing. He wore no hat, and just from his lesser size and hesitant body language, everyone could see it was the larger man who was in charge. Margie came out of the house wiping her hand on a towel. Sidwa followed, her hair now butter pecan colored ice cream dips all over her head making her look like a kewpie doll.

"Ma'am," said the large man, tipping the front brim of his hat up with just a finger push. "I'm Ryan Rondall, assistant fire chief with Colquitt County, and this is Edmund T. Petty." He motioned toward the other man who was folding the map and shaking his head. "Which one of you is Margaret Fontaine?"

"Why, that would be me?" With her newfound position of importance at being singled out by the striking Ryan Rondall, Margie stepped forward like a beauty contestant being called into a top ten line-up. "I'm sorry Mrs. Fontaine."

"Oh, that's Mizzz Fontaine. Mr. Fontaine is no longer in the picture."

"Ms. Fontaine, I'm afraid I have some bad news for you. We received word from the Lowndes County Fire Department that there was a fire at your place this afternoon One of your neighbors gave the fire department the number of Mrs. Sidwa Dean. Said she was your sister. Mr. Petty here tried to phone you a number of times, but there was always a busy signal, so we came out to tell you." He pointed a thumb down the street. "Missed your house."

Sidwa stepped forward with her wet curls drooping. "Leonard was feeling dyspeptic this morning, so we didn't go to church. We were here all day."

"833-8273?" said Edmund, fidgeting with a slip of paper.

"8237," said Sidwa.

Fireman Rondall whipped his head around to Edmund T. Petty with an expression of pure irritation.

"I'm dyslexic ma'am," said Edmund T. Petty, folding the map which he held upside down. "Been that way all my life. We went to ninety-six Shotsdale. Your sister here lives at. . .uh." Edmund T. Petty began unfolding the map again. "This is only my second week on the job," he added.

"Sixty-nine. I'm sixty-nine," said Sidwa.

"I'm sorry Ms. Fontaine. We came as quick as we could," said Edmund T. Petty, his last word trailing off.

Margie remained stunned at the news. She began rubbing her right hand over her knuckles, the bones making blue white knots against her palm. "How bad was it?"

"From what Chief Buckley said, it was a more than fifty percent loss," said Ryan Rondall. Margie dropped to her knees, losing one green pump as she sat down on her right hip. Sidwa kneeled beside her and put an arm around Margie's shoulders.

"It's too early for an official cause to be declared yet, but it appears to have started in the kitchen. Were you cooking this morning, Ms. Fontaine?"

"Rice Krispies. Gawdamn Rice Krispies." With that Margie sunk all the way to the floor. The last thing she saw was the flickering sun through the wisteria vine, its shady side blackened against the brilliant haze of June sunlight.

Robert Stewart

A Ploughed Field

A black thorn bush is rare as an ally.
So it is tonight, as cold hard
rain
softens our stiff hide
backed up against
the Sabbath Hill
as we gaze down on Haugh's field.
There, by the ploughman's intransigent board,
straight drills, like earthen hope,
fall in
over happed up cut seed
as the night soil rises
wave upon wave
as if signalling
life.

Alison Jennings

Apple Tree in Blossom (for John Locke)

If I ignore the reference to a fateful Tree of Knowledge,

this apple tree resembles what I picture as Paradise,
surrounding me in fragrant, lush, deep-colored haze –

Such sensory overload! Receptors malfunction, wires
cross: I'm breathing in the petals' nectar taste (plums,
or maybe pomegranate?) as they flutter sweetly down.

Other-worldly, swirling mists are rising from the blooms;
a balmy breeze is drifting from a distant ocean of perfume.

Pinkness is enfolding me in soft cocoons of cotton candy.

What audacity, as Nature nonchalantly shows her season's
wares, little caring if hearts leap up and leave us breathless
with desire for what is fleeting, and cannot be possessed.

Meli Broderick Eaton

Bird House

Deep
inside a box inside
a notch inside the spine
of a long tilting tree lie
the tender remains of a small nest.
The birds who built it
have flown, leaving behind
feather, function, purpose
all their intentions.

The window into its reedy center is the same
as the hole right through my heart
that pumps, pumps, squeezes life
and lets it flow. If you put your ear right up next to
this cleft, my heart, you might hear
thump-echo
      thump-echo
           thump—

…this is when memory speaks and we are suspended
together, kindred in the sanctuary of what we knew
revisiting this temple as if it's our religion and
offering recollection as reverence, tithing in tears

thump-echo
The heart flutters back into its chamber
because it must, if I am to stay
pressed faster to catch up to now
      thump-echo
I keep that space open
           thump-echo
for when you return
to this place, your flown ghost resurrected
      thump-echo

long enough to whisper into the box inside
a notch inside the spine of a long tilting tree
and we remember
thump
        echo
we remember

Catherine Moore

Not Fit for Circus Animals

Rattlesnake Lair—don't take a long stretch of imagination to figure what kind of folks lived down that road. Hazel Wallace idled in his car at the turn off Highway 28.

It was rare that he traversed to this end of Burnt Springs. But Fletcher Norris had called him—*couldn't talk over the phone—would he drop by Fletch's auto center?* Truthfully, Hazel hadn't known that Fletch owned a bona fide shop, he thought of his campaign manager more as a shade tree mechanic. With his bid for the sheriff's office floundering, Hazel was intent on ideas to improve his state of affairs—everything being worth consideration.

"Hang on kids, this should be an adventure."

Mason and Mabel hoorayed in the back seat, chanting, "Go daddy go."

Hazel drove slowly down the dirt road until a pair of loose dogs ran at the car, jumping and biting at the door handles. The canines dropped chase before the Norris Automotive sign. The Jeep Cherokee dipped as the drive continued into a gully, about thirty feet deep and blanketed in kudzu. The weed-ridden drive wound down through heaps of junked cars. *Fletch's place resembles a scrapyard.*

Reaching the bottom, Hazel noticed a silhouette at the top of the ravine—a peacock. In a flash, more of the great birds emerged. The children trembled at the noise of the dozen or so peafowl charging over the ridge and surrounding the car. They squealed *Daadeeeee.* When a peacock flew on the hood, Hazel got nervous. The peacock brandished his tiara of jeweled feathers, like a fan dancer on Bourbon Street, and cocked his brilliant colored neck backwards screeching.

"Keep your seat belts on," Hazel said to his children, illogically.

The agitated peacock stomped his scrawny legs scratching

the Jeep with his claws. "Git your buzzard body off there," Fletcher said, coming through the shop doorway with a shotgun. He fired a blank into the air and the peafowl scattered. Fletcher laughed. "When they came running at ya a banshee shrieking, betcha wanted to run."

Hazel rolled down his window, "Hunker down and take cover was more like it. Now, I hope it's safe for the kids." Hazel looked irritated but started directing his children to unload.

"They ain't overly aggressive, though, they do lunge and sport their talons. I figure would-be-thieves will tuck tail."

"Most people get themselves a guard dog, Fletch, but I guess it takes all kinds," Hazel said and slammed his door.

"Well, you never heard of the Dog Bite Law. The state's made it damn near impossible to have guard dogs without getting your pants sued off. I got rid of the pit-bulls 'cuz of the grief and bought some of these from Ruby Mae. Landed a deal with the old Hagan widow for them. Started with three—a cock and two hens—and look now."

"Ain't nature grand?" Hazel opened the back Jeep door to get his kids.

"It hasn't been easy keeping them alive. The neighbor's got his vermin running around 24/7, and there's not much in the way of grass in the auto lot so I have to supplement with feed."

Mabel wrapped her arms around her daddy's leg while he lifted Mason out of the car seat. "Sounds like an expense," Hazel said.

"Well, there are cheaper ways for sure. My brother-in-law keeps offering me the dregs from his delivery truck, but I won't let my peafowl eat peanut scum. I don't even think it's fit for circus animals, and I told him so," Fletcher said looking around. "Come inside where we can talk." A grease-covered mechanic walked out of a repair bay and rubbernecked the arrivals.

Fletcher placed the shotgun on brackets above his desk. "Surprised to see you with the kids in tow."

"What's that supposed to mean?" Hazel demanded. In his mind, Fletcher had a way of making observations that seemed like judgment.

Fletcher shrugged, dipped from a pouch of tobacco, chewed slow.

Hazel looked out the window. The peafowl still squabbled outside, but wandered off into the forest of abandoned cars. Irritated, he stroked his goatee. "Trouble with the missus. And money. Had to let the nanny go."

"Huh, perfect timing for our conversation. Like I said, my brother-in-law, Dewey, he drives for Crowley Brothers Nut Distributors. Picks up product over in Dothan, or maybe it's Troy, dunno, but he's running them down to Mobile for shipping."

"You called me out here to talk about peanut scum?" Hazel pointed his kids to the tattered plaid couch against the side office wall. There was a large glass window to the repair shop behind it. Hazel mused it wasn't likely that any customer sat there to wait on their vehicle.

"No, I want to meet about the latest super food. It's nuts. Couple their omega-3 fatty acid profile with their low glycemic index and the health gurus are going ape shit over them. Which, of course, is driving up prices."

Hazel had learned there was a bit of brilliance in Fletcher's seemingly rambled conversations and remained quiet.

"Look, I promised you a way to bring a flush of cash into the campaign account and here's how I'll deliver." Fletcher took his seat behind the desk. "What I'm really talking about here is the stock market. Not mutual funds—think commodities. The current trading on pecans yields four thousand dollars per ton. Your average truck hauls about twenty-two tons of nuts—we're looking at eighty-eight thousand dollars a delivery."   Hazel remained standing but leaned against a dusty bookcase housing repair manuals. "But your brother-in-law transports peanuts?"

"Mostly. Near holiday times, the nut distributors need to increase shipments of pecans. And with Alabama producing over six million pounds of them, that's a lot of cash crop rolling around on our highways."

Hazel whistled. "Continue." He gestured sit-down at his son Mason who had stood up on the couch to gain a better view through the repair shop window.

"On a recent delivery job, my brother-in-law was approached. There's an off-shore group interested in paying near market price but avoiding taxes and tariffs."

"Black market?"

"Essentially. But these aren't bad guys, just trying to make a living off international markets. Dewey called me because he needs drivers for the job—I used to haul for Garland Trucking. He doesn't want to be in the actual heist; only wants to report a truck theft. Handle the paperwork, and the questions, collect an unofficial end of the year bonus. The Christmas season is coming—he's got six kids."

The Wallace children began jumping on the couch at the mention of Christmas. The men ignored them, so the children linked hands and jumped faster.

"We 'take' the truck at a designated location. Dewey will file the shipment as stolen. The recipient is okay with the cargo being reported because even if arrested they post bail and regroup later. Simply the cost of a scam for them—their ship's already out at sea."

"And Dewey's cut?"

"Ten percent."

Hazel caught hold of Mabel when she fell from the couch, nearly landing in an old brass spit jar on the floor, which began to interest her. Hazel picked up the offending spittoon and handed it to Fletcher who moved it behind the desk.

"Not as dangerous as it sounds, Hazel. It requires no guns. No great hijinks. We'll be done before Dewey's loss report is filed." Fletcher paused to use the spittoon himself. "There's a bunch more trade out on Mobile Bay than anyone is aware of—cops don't question anything unless it's reported."

Hazel watched his kids climb back up on the couch and giggle at the window as if the whole world was their delight. They shouted *bang, bang,* cocking their thumbs pistol-poised. "Now this is an interesting proposition, for a choir-boy like yourself. What happened to thou shalt not steal, Fletch?"

"I'm beginning to realize that as a lot of hardline hooey, in interpretation, of course. One fellow's misery is another fellow's gain—that's the way the world has always been." Fletcher's eye twitched uncontrollably. "And make no mistake, companies write off costs like this every day."

"So, you're talking eighty-eight K to drive a truck from one location to another?"

"Bingo! Half-a-day's work. We simply run it from red clay to the gulf sands." He placed his hand against the throbbing eye.

"Sounds easy, though I can't be a party to this while running for office. I understand the risk seems low, but if I was caught near that shipping truck there's no reasonable explanation for me being there." Hazel glanced outside, then over at the shop window, as if checking for eavesdroppers. "It's an ingenious plan, Fletch, I just can't be your boots on the ground. I sense that Sheriff Boone's put a tail on me."

"Okay. I'll find someone else."

"Bergeron, again?"

"Hey, the guy keeps his mouth shut. And is good in a pinch."

Hazel nodded. "Well, I'll let you get back to your rat killing." He scooped his kids off the couch heading for the door.

"But the money, I can still run this through our campaign account, right?" Fletcher asked.

*

Kelley Bergeron relaxed in his usual way: shirtless, boxers not briefs, and a cold beer in hand. Fletcher sat on Bergeron's bar stool in a tidy kitchen with vintage pennants tattooed on its beige manufactured walls, a collection that centered around a prized but faded Louisiana World Expo 1984 pennant. He stared at the felt wall art as he finished describing the next potential endeavor.

"Sure, sure, I got a cousin dat can help us out, too," said Kelley.

"You seem to always have a cousin to rustle up, Kell."

"It's a hazard of bayou living. Back home, da landscape is so purdy everyone's falling in love and fornicating." Kelley grinned in a way that looked like he wanted to be somewhere else. Doing something else.

"Well, we don't need anyone additional for this one. Just you and me," Fletcher said.

"Keep shares down—good thinking. And what's dat share?"

"Five thousand."

"*Bien*, I'm in. Another voodoo?" Kelley tossed Fletcher a beer from the fridge.

*

Fletcher handed Kelley Bergeron a crimson colored thermal mug as he slid behind the wheel. They were in his neighbor's pickup but had switched drivers on account of Bergeron not being 'a morning person.'

Though Kelley was grateful for the hot coffee inside, he shriveled up his nose, "Roll Tide? *Non*." He fished around the floor of his truck and come up with large styrofoam cup imprinted with Suwanee Swifty, underneath flew a silhouette of a long-winged bird, black against a yellowed sun. The cup rim looked like it had been chewed, but Kelley open the mug and poured his coffee in, tipping the drink mocking, "Padna." He sipped as Fletcher drove along the dirt rise they called a road.

First dawn appeared, then vanished back into the dark alluvial plains east of the Burnt River, once bogland now overtaken with wax myrtle and loblolly pine. A few houses sprang up as they entered Chiggers Grove. They caught a red light on the town square.

"Figures," Fletcher said. He briefly considered driving through the only signaled intersection in the county, but with the courthouse looming to the right, he thought better.

"Are they ever gonna fix dat hole?" Kelley pointed in the direction of some weathered barricades, with traffic flashers, out on the courthouse lawn. "Would be nice to sit under a shady tree."

"Folks are spooked by it."

"By da hole? Or by shade?"

Fletcher grinned. "See that old pecan tree? With the long limb toward the courtroom door? They used to hang people there, directly after trial. No appeals back in those days."

Kelley whistled low and long. "You know some innocent folks got to have swung on dat limb."

"Maybe. When I was young, my mama would warn me from playing under there. She was crazy superstitious."

"*Mais oui*, sounds like a smart woman. So, now everybody is spooked by da tree?"

"Yes and no. A couple of decades ago, that sinkhole underneath opened up. Right after the bicentennial. Over the years, they've tried to fill that hole with dirt and debris, tar and bricks, but the next morning the hole is always swept out clean."

"Holy mother of haints." Kelley swore.

"It's the work of vandals, for coonsakes."

Kelley made the sign of the cross.

"You don't believe in ghosts, do you? I thought you were a God-fearing man." Fletcher sounded disgusted.

"I am. And I'm afraid God sends some back. Or refuses to take some in." Kelley kept his eye on the side-mirror, watching for uninvited ride-hitchers as they drove away. "Some souls don't rest."

In a flash they were out of the county seat, back rolling down Highway 28 where the faded road stripes reappeared along with the morning sun.

"Like my papa, my very own *père*, for instance."

Fletcher threw him a look.

"Started right after he died. Yeah, *Père* was so full of drink, his body burned for three days at da crematory. He was bright and blue, and no one could figure how to get that flame out. Crematory operator never seen anything like it. He called Father Landry, who gave da flame its last rites, hoping this would encourage *Père* to go yon, ya know?" Kelley nodded at Fletcher trying to establish agreement on the facts.

"*Mais*, no. Dat body still burned like a Moses bush. 'Must be a miracle,' Father Landry says to ma *mère*. And then, come to find out, didn't she have the bishop himself on the phone within an hour? She was thinking beatification, ya know? Like *Père* was some sort of saint." Kelley laughed. "Bless his soul, many things he was, but not dat. Prolly wanted to stick around for a last *fais do-do*."

Kelley leisurely lit a cigarette from the pack of smokes in his pocket. He studied the embered end. "Somewhere *Père's* spirit still burns, like canned Sterno, forever blue. At someone's party, no less."

Fletcher bit his lower lip, not wanting to disrespect the dead. Or his friend's story. Kelley rambled on with another tale chosen to support his case for the existence of ghosts, this time it featured his dear departed *Tante* Monique and that rascal of a character in every good cajun tale—come-to-find-out.

For the rest of the ride, Bergeron alternated between full-on chatter and snoring. Fletcher didn't mind the quieter moments, taking in the landscape as they left behind the cypress, oak, and sweetgum, moving into hills of short-leaf pine, and later wide peanut fields. He loved this country.

After driving into the rising sun since dawn, they turned south outside of Troy. The sign marker read Highway 231. "Yup, that's the Flora-Bama Parkway," Fletcher said.

"Flora-Bama? Pee-o! Y'all have some funny talk round here."

"Yeah, WE do. As long as you reside here, Kell, you should soak up some Flora-Bama fun. At least take in the Mullet Toss."

Kelley slicked back his hair.

"Not that mullet—the fish." Fletcher spat into his ready cup. "It's a competition for the distance one can toss a mullet from the Florida border into Alabama."

Like any good Mardi-Gras veteran, Kelley held a skeptical outlook on this described fun factor. Most folks, in his estimation, didn't know how to have fun like the cajuns.

"Big name country music stars come down and play. Can't be all that bad," Fletcher said.

They argued entertainment values for nearly a half hour and came on a crossroads with a Flying J, still lit in a blaze of fluorescents, even well after sun up.

"That's the truck stop," Fletcher said with sudden gravity.

Catty-corner to the Flying J, a boxy diner perched up on a hill. The purple and orange lettering somewhat faded—King Waffle—it looked to be a Huddle House knock-off.

"Let's get some grub and talk through this, one last time," said Fletcher turning off the highway.

A sticker—Smoke 'Em If Ya Got 'Em—greeted them at the front door and the diner smelled of bacon and cigarette; its air conditioner wheezed trying to keep pace with the haze.

Fletcher studied the room instead of the menu. Everything, from the walled plastic pictures of food to the number of customers ordering 'the usual,' read as local. He hoped they didn't stand out. *Kelley Bergeron didn't help.* Lighting up his cajun smile along with a cigarette.

Kelley charmed the ladies, especially ones as attractive as the waitress, even if she was too young. "I'm hung-gar-ry, little lady, what comes on da King Waffle platter?"

"Blue shoo topping, love me tender tots, lonesome tonight egg any-style, and a side of jailhouse ham." She shifted on her hip.

"Ah, Elvis—I thought you was waffling for Jesus," said Kelley.

"Say what?" the waitress answered.

"Da King. Your sign," Kelley pointed his cigarette at the roadside, "WWJHFB?"

"What would Jesus have for breakfast?" Fletcher quietly added.

"Oh, that. You'd be looking for the Salvation Waffle, but we only serve that during Lent."

"Didja hear dat, Fletch? The Salvation is only available during Lent."

"Mmm..."

"Y'all should come on back then, 'cuz the Salvation is *real* good. Sprinkle toppings. Got the baby Jesus inside." The waitress jabbed her pen on the order pad for emphasis.

"Go on—da Jesus cake baby, like in a king cake?"

She nodded, with a vacant but sweet smile.

Kelley watched the line order cook pressing a waffle iron. Flip and re-press. "Got to be one small-ass baby Jesus to flatten like dat and not melt."

"Yeah." Fletcher turned to watch thoughtfully. "So small I'd probably figure I'd swallowed a filling, or an insect," he added looking around.

Kelley held up two fingers, "King Waffle platters?" Fletcher shrugged in agreement. The waitress poured coffee before leaving with their order.

Fletcher pointed to the grease-flecked wall and said, "This place could use a good cleaning. Hope the breakfast doesn't taste like prison food."

"I like how exacting you are, Fletch. But how would you know what prison food tastes like?"

Fletcher smiled. "If I'm going to be exacting, well, been meaning to ask you, Kell—how exactly do you make a living?"

"Resale."

Now Fletcher grinned.

"Not what you're thinking. I make my money on eBay."

"E what?" Fletcher asked.

"An auction house—over da web. Every other month I buy abandoned suitcases from Unclaimed Baggage, up in north 'Bama, and sell da contents on eBay." He shook four sugar packets, ripped them into his coffee. "Easy money. By da load."

"Seriously? What kinds of contents make that kind of money?"

"Rolexes. Formal gowns. Elk antlers. Imported wines all day long. Some stuff I don't sell." Kelley pulled the spoon out of his coffee. "Like boxes of condoms." He lifted his mug at his buddy.

Kell's something else. Fletcher's neighbor sure kept a low profile, but he wondered what kind of life Kelley really lived. *At least he's not a crook* that Fletcher originally assumed.

When the almost satisfactory meal was cleared, Fletcher pulled a fax from his pocket and laid a shipping manifest on the table. "Let's see, shipment control number, that's meaningless for us. Here, drivers-slash-crew: Smith, D. Won't you know it, there's two D Smiths? Um, destination ports, Dawson, Georgia. Nope. And Mobile, Alabama. Bingo. That's our D Smith's cargo. Now, the conveyance number will match the VIN on the truck—that's what Dewey told me."

Kelley picked up the pen left by the waitress along with their bill. "And that'll be on an ID plate on da cab, driver's side door," he said.

Fletcher nodded to Kelley, poised to make note on a napkin. "So we are looking for 2NE5SJ68K09." He looked at his watch. "And by now, Dewey will have it parked over at the Flying-J."

Fletcher and Kelley acted nonchalant as they walked the back parking lot of the truck stop, engaging in a lively conversation, laughing, to hide the preoccupation of looking. Once locating the designated rig among the many Crowley Nut trucks, they seemingly parted, each taking turns using the facilities. First Fletch, so Kelley could move his pickup closer to the nut truck. Later they switched positions; Kelley taking a smoke outside the rest room entrance as Fletcher shifted his stuff from the bed of the Chevy into the Crowley tractor-trailer. Kelley watched Fletcher throw in his mobile CB radio, an old army blanket, and a portable butane heater, then searched for keys under the floor mat before climbing in the cab.

"Planning on camping out?" Kelley shouted from his pickup.

"What? Oh, the Little Buddy? Dewey warned me the heat in the cab doesn't work worth a lick. Give me a second to get set up and we'll test the CB. Trying channel fifteen first." Fletcher closed the door and slid open the window. "What's your handle?"

"Give 'em Kell."

"That figures. Mine is Road Fish. "

Kelley made a face.

"It's a trucking for Jesus kind of thing." Fletcher explained, closing his window.

A couple minutes later, Kelley's CB speaker crackled.

"Break-one-five, radio check. This is Road Fish."

"Affirmative, Fisherman, hear ya loud and clear."

"Haven't driven one of these in over a decade. Gonna be an adventure, Give 'em Kell. Over." Fletcher sounded gleeful.

Catherine Moore **169**

"Before we drive this convoy outta here, you positive you got da right truck?"

Fletcher glanced at the bill of lading Dewey left on the dash. "Yup, it's destination Mobile. Over and out."

The difference between the Alabama and Florida Panhandle landscape was indiscernible—same patches of towering pine, surly red soil, peanut fields spread out like a great green oceans. Kelley took in a row of palm trees propped by wooden braces in front of cinderblock rest rooms and the requisite Highway Patrol car.

"How about it Fish Bandit—watch our back door—got a Smokey out taking pictures."

"That's a ten-four, Give 'em Kell."

One might miss the state welcome station, but not the series of lottery signs along the roadside. The cheap neon placards posted every three feet looked weathered and culminated with a large hand-painted image of a flamingo holding an arrow—TURN RIGHT NOW—LOTTO—KEGS. The artist failed to leave enough room for the correct neck length, which elicited comment from Kelley.

"Hey padna, they got pink ducks in these parts?"

"Negatory. But they got pink everything else down here, especially at the government office for voluntary taxes."

The parking lot was full, and half of the Sunshine Liquors' customers parked along the shoulder of Highway 231, forcing both trucks in the Burnt Springs convoy to slow down.

"Bama. Bama. Bama. Look at 'em lined up to hand Florida their money," Fletcher said in disgust.

"Tu-wee," Kelley whistled. "Sign says thirteen million jackpot—hope you don't think ill of me when I get me a ticket. Since we're rambling through anyhow."

There was a long pause. Kelley swatted the speaker on his CB unit to be sure the wires weren't crossed.

"Next pit stop, I'll turn a blind eye. Over," Fletcher said. He sped up. The faster they got through Florida and back in 'Bama, the better.

They made good time on Interstate-10 across the panhandle and rolled into Alabama again a little over two hours later. It wasn't long after the state line to the vista of Mobile Bay from the bridge into the port city.

"Break-one-five. Give 'em Kell, that's it on the right-hand side. We're here—Seabuilt Industries. Now to find Gate C-3. C-3. Over."

"Charlie *une-deux-trois*. Roger dat."

The shipping yard was double-fenced. One to border the outer thru-road and one as an interior fence enclosing the loading areas, which was guarded at its gate. Seeing the gate sign, Kelley pulled alongside the chain metal outer fence. They consolidated into one vehicle, leaving Bergeron's pickup outside, and drove the truck through the gate.

"Good afternoon, sir." Fletcher grabbed the shipping paperwork and handed it to the guard.

The young man was of slight build and of obvious Asian descent. Unsmiling, he gave them a quick nod. "Good day," he said with a thick accent and walked back into his booth. The guard consulted a log hanging on a clipboard on the rear wall, then waved their truck through. "Park." He pointed to an area against the fence inside the entry point. In front of them, were idling delivery trucks and a series of warehouses.

"Friendly," Kelley commented almost to himself.

They waited nearly fifteen minutes before they saw any other sign of life. And that sign moved slow. A large Asian man came out of a warehouse, the girth of his waist hung over his belt, jiggling as he walked toward them. The man struggled off balance by the weight of a briefcase carried in his left hand, but he switched hands halfway and made it to the driver's door. "You Fletcher?" he said, a smidge of Asia in his voice.

"Yeah, you Van?"

Van nodded and smiled. The briefcase swung at his side. He looked ready to heave it up, when a tall dark-skinned man emerged at the warehouse doorway. He waved his arms in great agitation, still clutching papers in his hands. "Attention! *Reviens ici!*"

"French?" said Fletcher.

Kelley nodded. "Vietnamese?" He added, watching the one named Van waddle his way back to the building, grappling with his case and calling out "*đến đây!*" to the gate guard.

The men had an animated conversation almost out of earshot. None of it sounded like English to Fletcher. He swiped his arm against his forehead. "C'mon," he said. "Just give us the cash and we're out of here."

Most of it don't sound very French, either. Kelley leaned out the window taking a smoke. "*Pistache?*" He pulled his head back in. "Vietnamese aren't da easiest to understand, but unless my French has gone ta hell, I think we may have hauled peanuts down with us."

"Peanuts? No, this rig's full of pecans." Fletcher reached for the dash, only to remember he had surrendered the paperwork.

Kelley sniffed the air like a hound. "Dat's not what I smell." He leaned out the window again. "And they sound pissed so they must be smelling da double-cross." He took a long drag. "Don't expect I can convince them we brought some fancy cajun pecans, do ya?"

"Kell, I've seen you talk the paint down off a house, but I don't know about this." Fletcher shook his head despondently. He felt his walleye cross and twitch.

"Was dat guard carrying a gun?"

"Oh, sweet Jesus. We're gonna be sucking the sorrow, aren't we?" Fletcher pressed his palm against his errant eye.

"I mean if he wasn't carrying, this would be da time to drop everything and bolt. Was he?" Kelley pointed his cigarette at Fletcher.

"I don't know. I don't think…"

The dock men cut their conversation and moved at the truck.

"Go!" Kelley said. He jumped down out of the cab and Fletcher followed suit, racing toward the gate opening behind them. They heard the guys shouting. As they ran to the pickup, they both expected to hear gunshots in-between their pumping heartbeats. It never came. Halfway to his Chevy, Kelley glanced over his shoulder to see flames inside the truck. He faltered.

"What?" Fletcher stopped too.

The foreigners pulled at a hose at the side of the warehouse, yelling directions at each other.

"Damn. Must not have put out my cig."

Roaring, the fire burst through the cab and rolled outward, shattering the windshield. The explosion echoed between buildings.

"The heater," said Fletcher. They looked at each other, then bolted again.

Inside the safety of their pickup, they saw the truck still ablaze, spreading to the cargo container, down and along the top.

"Peanuts," they said together.

"Dat's some kindling we don't want to stick around for." Kelley threw the Chevy into gear.

Fletcher had promised a side trip to the infamous Flora-Bama Bar on the way home from the heist. In a less celebratory mood, they settled for Cooter Bob's outside of Chiggers Grove. The loud honky-tonk music was a foil to the silent ride back. Fletcher had never seen Kelley like this, saying little else after leaving Mobile. "*Mais*, Fletch, maybe it's for da best."

"Hard to figure, Kell." Fletcher rode the rest of the way without inviting conversation.

Two hours later, they still hadn't much to say. Hugging a couple of cold Budweisers, the would-be bandits sat at the bar ignoring most of its activity. Kelley asked for the food menu, since Fletcher had taken the bowl of free peanuts and shoved it away.

"La, what's dat?" Kelley pointed at the TV.

The bartender looked up at the muted set and said, "Massive fire down in Mobile. Dockside. Lots of cargo lost." The keep dried a glass while looking at the screen. "A shame. Hope that's not someone's Christmas in flames."

The footage zoomed in on a white-hot warehouse burning.

Fletcher put his head down on the bar top.

Kelley stared into the blue light of the TV screen. "*Père*," he said.

Katherine Burnette

A Mother's Prayer

I hate the phone. I turn it down when the television is on, when other voices fill the room, leaking into the cracks and crevices. When it rings, I mutter a prayer that it's not you or, at least, not someone calling about you. About your broken body on a gurney with stitches undulating across your shaved head; or worse, you long limbed and silent in the cooler at the morgue.

Grief hugs me like a sloth with long arms. It gets so heavy sometimes that I have to tip it off my shoulders and onto the sofa. It judges me with its large liquid eyes. But, it always climbs back on, usually when I'm not looking.

I cannot go to church anymore. All of the prayers that I have prayed for you are waiting at the door. The blues, greens, and reds from the apostles in the stained glass illuminate the wispy lacy things. Floating in with me, the prayers get louder, arguing, murmuring. They fight amongst themselves. I cannot hear the sermon.

You mourn your lost love and I mourn your prophesized passing. I'd cross the river and use my lips to puff life's air down her scored throat if it would keep you here one day longer. But I cannot fight the dead. She is frozen in your heart, young and beautiful. You are frozen in mine, aged three, white blond and chortling a deep laugh.

Does your heroin numb your feelings as well as my daily goblets of dark red wine? Does it smell of dank earth and summer blackberries and give you what you need to face the morning? I always hope that morning won't come, that I don't have to remember and with remembering want to die. But, not dying because you still live.

If the phone rings, I won't answer. I'll turn my head from the sloth's obsidian eyes and close my ears to the music of old prayers, each note lit by God's light. I will sink down into the stained sofa, hugging my glass, and turning the volume of the television up louder.

Jonathan Greenhause

The house had no windows

but possessed doors through which to see,
lacked ceilings

but never suffered rain.
The walls were imaginary, constructed

with suspect pillars of belief,
& the basement

was left unfinished,
comprised of a hole with a single step.

The attic was mythically suspended
upon a missing base,

the basic bathrooms
cardboard boxes & foraged leafs,

the bedrooms decidedly puritan,
only permitting sleep.

Guests were treated
as valuable prisoners, consented

to return invitations. Tax collectors
pled for nothing,

the ornery mailman
delivered solely junk, Jehovah's Witnesses

slept fitfully, grouped by the doorbell,
& Avon called

but – fond of pranks –

subsequently hung up. The kitchen

stored mildewed utensils, rotten food,
& tiny closets

simply contained space
for the concept of themselves. Shelves

collapsed from dust's accumulation,
yet the homeowners

were unwary, blissful,
found nothing eerie with this hovel

lovingly built; though, admittedly,
they resided overseas.

Michael J O'Connor

Hold Up Your Purse!

Even though it was May, there was rain pounding down on the metal roof of the theater's outdoor smoking area, and I sat on the concrete floor, shaking. The weekend of shows had taken its toll on me. I had never acted before, and when I agreed to be in my friend's play, I hadn't realized how terrifying it would be, and how high I would get off of it. Coming down after each show proved impossible, and I had taken to keeping the buzz going with cheap bourbon long after the final bow. This was, of course, after getting a buzz going in the first place in order to stave off the fear. The fear was always there just as long as there were people out there that I couldn't escape. For the moment, though, I could hide in the smoking area, lighting cigarette after cigarette until the stage manager came to tell me there was ten minutes until show time.

"Thank you, ten," I replied without looking up from lighting my last cigarette.

I stared ahead and shivered. My shoes scuffed on the ground, echoing off of the building and coming right back to me, spinning in my ears for a second time. This was the fourth and final show of the weekend, and I had found myself out there before every single one of them. Before the previous shows, I had my plastic bottle of bourbon with me out there, taking gulps and leaning into the cool air. When the thought of the dark room and the faces and the lights would seep from my brain down into my stomach, I would take another swig and let the acid from the bourbon cut the alkaline bubbling of nerves down there. Before long I would be flexing my biceps and pounding on my chest, ready to take on the dark room and the faces and the lights; ready to make them feel again. On this night, though, I sat on the floor and shook while rain water collected on the metal roof and crashed down onto the street below. I puffed at the cigarette, but it had gone out, and I didn't even try to relight it. I flicked it out over the railing and let it fall with the rain water into the gutter.

When the stage manager came out to tell me there were five minutes until show time now, I was already getting up.

"Thank you, five," I said, groaning and creaking.

"Are you gonna be okay out there?" he asked.

"Yeah, why?"

"You look like death warmed over, man. I'm surprised you're even standing."

I caught a glimpse of myself in the window.

"Well, thanks for the pep talk, I appreciate it."

"I'm just saying," he continued as I patted him on the shoulder and walked inside.

"Thank you so much."

I was gripped by fear. I had chosen to stay straight for this performance because I wanted to see if I could. Even though I had never messed up explicitly because of the bourbon in any of the shows, I had gotten a little bit overzealous with my performance. The play broke the fourth wall and involved the audience quite a bit. On Friday night I got particularly expressive with my "p" sounds during a monologue addressing the front row and watched a man wipe my spit from his eyes as I chattered on. I had also gotten too over-the-top while jumping into the arms of one of my fellow actors, Charles. The joke was that I was six foot five and two hundred and twenty pounds and Charles was very small. If I jumped gently enough, he could hold me, but if I was out of my mind on rot gut bourbon and stage fright, it was a different story. That story ended with Charles having to spend the rest of the night and the next day icing his back for a slipped disc.

I walked down the hall and turned into the area behind the curtain. I could hear the low hum of the audience talking and the sweat started dripping down my back. Charles was standing next to the curtain holding an ice pack onto his back. I pointed at him.

"Sorry, again."

He gave me an unamused look and went back to staring at

the floor. The third actor in the play, Rebecca, was waiting there with him, and we all stood with our arms crossed, telling ourselves whatever prayers were necessary. I could feel the skin on my arms starting to tingle, and my brain started flooding. It sputtered and spun in all different directions and I felt for the small plastic bottle of whiskey but felt nothing. I was outside of the spaceship with no rope to hold onto, falling backwards into the sky. I held my hand against the wall to steady myself and caught Rebecca and Charles looking at me. They hadn't seen me drinking anything the entire night, and they must have imagined that I moved on to something much more sinister. I had been so open about my vices that when they saw me with nothing, their imaginations began working for them and they started to listen for secret pill bottles and look for loose syringes to fall out of my pockets. What could I possibly be up to?

I suddenly couldn't get warm. I was shivering and my teeth were chattering.

"What is up with you?" said Rebecca, eyeing me up and down.

"Nothing, I'm just cold, aren't you guys cold?"

"I'm sweating my ass off and I have an ice pack," said Charles. "Thanks, by the way."

I slipped around the corner and talked myself down, shivering and chattering when the stage manager walked past me and patted me on the back.

"Lights. Break a leg out there," he said.

"Don't encourage him," said Charles.

I wanted to run, but there was nowhere to run, so I slipped back behind the curtain, and waited for the lights to go down. That was when my mouth started going numb.

When the curtain opened, I was able to get my first couple of lines out okay, and thought that maybe there was a chance that I would get through this. Every time I started thinking that, though, my brain would tell me to run as fast as I could. I started trying to come up with some sort of line to make my exit make sense, but nothing was presenting itself and my brain was spinning. While I was trying to get my focus back, I noticed that everyone was looking at me. Charles and Rebecca were standing in their spots on stage and were staring wild eyed and terrified at my confused face. I couldn't figure out where we were and I started to dart for the curtain, but Charles broke the silence.

"Well, what do you think?" he said, widening his eyes even more.

I stood frozen.

"Somebody say something!" Rebecca yelled.

I remembered a line. Not the line that I was supposed to say, but a line that was at least in the same play. We picked it up from there, and Charles and Rebecca directed every ounce of hate from their eyes right on me for the next couple of scenes.

My mouth was still tensed up, and my hands were tingling, but my heart wasn't pounding like it had been. My voice was still shaking, but it seemed like I was going to at least be able to finish the performance without running away, down the stairs and into the alley, never to be seen or heard from again. The stench of my mistake was still in the air, though. I didn't know where we were or how far ahead we had skipped. I was fairly certain that there were improvised parts of the play coming up, and I wanted to try and redeem myself somewhat for my panicky screw up. Rebecca went into the audience to start her improvised piece, and I settled toward the back of the stage with Charles, our hands placed on our knees and our heads attentive to what was happening up in the seats.

Rebecca walked up the stairs into the grandstand style seats and stood among the faces that stared back at her and us. She turned around and began delivering her lines. I started feeling better, like things were finally turning around and that I had gotten the dead weight and tingly feeling off of my back. I couldn't say the same for Charles, who had a look of pain in his eyes as he tried to keep his bent-over position. Rebecca got to the point in her lines where she had to pick someone out of the audience and get them to hold up an item they had. I watched her scan the aisles up and down until she came across two women seated on the end, with pleasant smiles and willing faces.

"Here," Rebecca said, "hold up your purse!"

The woman seated right on the end looked back at her blankly. She blinked and Rebecca laughed softly.

"Hold up your purse!"

The woman sat and nodded, her face was still open and giving.

"Hold up your purse!"

Charles and I started laughing and exchanged glances. A lot can happen in theater when audience participation is introduced, and it's not always great, but Rebecca was a competent, skillful performer, and we were certain she would find a creative, funny way out of this.

"Come on, hold up your purse!"

The woman just smiled and nodded. That was when a horrible thought came to me, and I was panicked and shrieking on the inside all over again.

"Hold up your god damned purse," Rebecca said, doubling down for comedic effect. This time the woman pointed to her ear as she smiled and nodded.

"Oh god," I whispered.

"Come on, hold it up, what is wrong with you!?"

"What is it?" Charles whispered.

"Hold up your purse! Are you stupid or something?"

"No," I whispered to Charles, "She's deaf."

Charles and I just stayed frozen at the back of the stage, our hands resting on our knees, and Charles' back starting to give out. It was like watching a person about to walk off the edge of a building, we were helpless and she was oblivious. She began berating the woman.

"Jesus, what is wrong with you!? Can't you understand simple instructions, hold up your god damn purse!"

I looked at Charles and my eyes pleaded with him to help her, to do something. My mouth was now fully numb and couldn't even open. I was trying to catch my breath, but I couldn't. As Rebecca laid into this poor woman, I began to see some of the faces in the crowd start to put the pieces together on what was happening. They were all starting to catch on, and I watched a wave of understanding and awkward sympathy emanate out from the center of the theater. Rebecca was right there in the middle of it, happily playing in the eye of the hurricane.

As she continued, the woman's friend put her hand on Rebecca's arm as she went to grab the purse. She pointed forcefully at her ear and then the woman's ear and then shook her head. Rebecca stood and watched, and finally the truth of the situation started to dawn on her. It was like she turned around and the hurricane was right in front of her. There was a look of resignation in her eyes that you usually only see in people who have just been sentenced to life in prison. Once she realized this woman was deaf and that she had been calling her an idiot for the last five minutes, we all stood still in silence. Everyone in the audience and the crew and us actors on the stage all took a moment to reevaluate what we were doing with our lives. We were all sitting in a dark room watching a woman berate a deaf person. It was eerie and surreal.

Rebecca moved on as best as she could, but every bit of socially constructed magic had been sucked out of the room, and everybody just wanted it to end so they could pour out into the street and move on with their lives. We moved through the rest of the lines quickly, and when we were done, the audience politely clapped, but it was obvious they didn't feel that good about doing so. Charles limped off the stage and put his melting ice pack directly back on his lower back. We stood backstage and looked at each other for a second. I pulled out a cigarette and put it in my mouth.

"Sorry about skipping those lines," I said, and I slipped around the corner to the smoking area.

I smoked the cigarette as quickly as I could, and tried to breathe in as much cold air as I could. There was a fine mist in the air and I took it all into my chest like a shipwrecked man kissing the shore. It stung my lungs and made me cough. I went downstairs and stood in the lobby of the theater. No one else from the audience wanted to make eye contact with me, and I couldn't blame them. It was best if we all just forgot the night ever happened, and if any of us saw each other on the street, we would pretend we didn't recognize each other; but we would always remember.

I saw Rebecca walk through the lobby and outside. She leaned into a doorway out on the street, and try to light a cigarette. I handed her my lighter.

"I didn't know you smoked," I said.

"I don't."

She lit the cigarette and shook her head as she blew out the smoke. Her eyes were big and watery in the street lights.

"Hey that was really not that bad, it was pretty funny," I said.

The surface tension of her tears broke, and they started to stream down her face.

"It was just awful," she said, putting her hands over her face.

"No, really, it was fine I promise."

I lit a cigarette of my own and we stood there smoking until we heard footsteps coming up and a figure appeared around the corner of the doorway. It was the woman who wouldn't hold up her purse.

"Oh god," Rebecca said, trying to wipe her tears away quickly.

The woman's face was still bright and cheerful, and she leaned forward, grabbing Rebecca's arm. She nodded and smiled directly at her and squeezed, then reached into her purse and pulled out a tissue for her. She smiled a goodbye at us and we watched her walk down the street. The mist in the air seemed to completely envelop her as she got smaller and farther away, and I like to think that just before she completely disappeared from view she held her purse high above her head like a trophy, just out of reach for us to see.

Charles came out onto the street and asked me for a cigarette, which I lit for him and put in his mouth so he wouldn't have to let go of his ice pack.

"Who needs a drink?" he said.

The three of us walked off in the same direction my parents and the deaf woman with the purse had walked in, and we laughed and filled the street with our cries of "hold up your purse" out into the night sky. It bounced off the buildings and swirled into the open windows above us. There were no more faces in a dark room that we had to make smile and there were no more backstage areas to pace and pray in. The fight was over and we hadn't won, but we were still walking, we were still shouting and laughing, and we were still alive.

Dawn Terpstra

Gentle thunder

growls in low farewell,
like a distant horn

on a ship sailing slowly
through billowing headlands.

I see you jump, laughing
beneath the pruning shake

of a lilac branch, captive
drops tumble. Fragrant goblets

pour showers upon your head,
sun-touched tears trickle past

time-trenched wrinkles,
those I love to trace.

In blue eyes
I see it smiling,

wet kiss of spring.

Joyce Schmid

Sunset From the Top of Twin Peaks

San Francisco

Because there is no other thing to do,
I give permission for the day to pass,
this day with you when we are young,
as we have been for such a long, long time
our hair has turned to precious metal,
and some Dutch master has illuminated us
with fine-drawn pencil lines.

Because there is no other way,
I give permission for the lava-stream
of headlights along Market Street to flow,
for buildings going pink with Alpenglow
to shine, for pearls festooned along the bridge
to Berkeley to light up across the Bay,
anticipating dusk.

Because there is no other thing to do,
I turn toward the west
and give permission for the sun to fall
toward its gold reflection in the ocean
as I stand with you and watch it sink,
and cool to red,
and disappear.

Patricia Slaga

Makin' Do

I can still hear Mama calling me from the front room: "Patsy, when you finish with those rubber bands, put them back in the drawer!" My brother and I had been making "crawlers" by using broken pieces of crayons, empty thread spools and rubber bands. We would thread the rubber bands through the hole in the spool and anchor with a crayon on each end. Then, by winding the crayon and setting the spool free, it would inch forward on the table until the band unwound completely. We would do this over and over entertaining ourselves, seeing whose crawler went further – sort of an early version of Matchbox cars. Times were hard and bought toys were in short supply during the 1940's.

Mama was a "saver". She saved everything! In her words, "You never know when you might find a use for it!" She had a rubber band ball, a string ball, and a ball of used aluminum foil. God forbid that anyone would throw anything away that might someday "come in handy". She lived by that rule. We often made light of her habit of putting things back, but more than likely we would someday come up against a dilemma, and Mama's drawer had just the thing we needed.

Mama had three daughters, then a son. The son died at six-months of age. In rural North Carolina at that time, doctors who made house calls were also in short supply. There was only one within a twenty-five mile radius that was known to drive his old jalopy down long winding farm roads to attend to the sick. He always had with him a little black bag that held all he presumed he would ever need. There was no such thing as health insurance, and often the doctor would be paid with a chicken or loaf of homemade bread. This old doc came to our family emergency-- and showed up drunk. Sadly, another area where "makin do" came into play.

The baby died shortly after and the doctor signed the death certificate as "Meningitis". Sometime later, the baby's four-year-old sister confessed she had shared her baked corn with him. In all probability, he choked to death. In his drunken state, the doctor had put down a random diagnosis.

Mama went on to have two more daughters and another son. Six children to raise on a laborer's salary .... so, nothing was ever wasted. Old clothes not wearable were never discarded until we first snipped off all the buttons for the button jar. Broken shoestrings could be used to hold just about anything together. Cardboard was a premium. Daddy used the good corrugated type to line our shoes when holes appeared in the soles. This happened more frequently than we care to remember, seeing as how shoes were passed down from one sister to a younger sister or brother, and in light of the fact that we walked wherever we had to go.

Daddy never learned to drive, never owned a car. He rode public transit system to town, where he worked at RJ Reynolds Tobacco Company as a machinist. When he retired, he was given a banquet, that included a gift of sterling silver place setting for twelve. He had worked there forty years with perfect attendance! Once he almost had to stay home from work when he seriously cut his lower leg with an ax while chopping wood. Wrapped in ripped strands from a bed sheet, he went to work, then going for treatment and stitches after quitting time. Daily, he walked a mile and a quarter to the bus-stop by the school. Occasionally, during bad weather, a neighbor would give him a lift to the bus-stop. We walked that same distance to school, and like Daddy, covered the same distance when we walked back home. Church was almost as far, and we rarely missed church in favorable weather.

You see, back in the 40's the country was dealing with the affects of war. Many commodities were in short supply as much was being used for war effort. Jobs were affected as men were drafted. Folks would hold on to what was useful in the event a necessity would arise and availability of such was scarce, even if one had the money to buy, which was highly unlikely. When a body needed something they didn't have, they had to "make do" with what they had. That's what Mama always said. Hence the phrase *"Makin' do"*.

Once I received a "tongue lashing" for taking paraffin and rolling it in sugar to make homemade chewing gum. I was caught "red-handed" hiding under the table enjoying my sweet treat. Chewing gum was a rare pleasure, but like many other things, fell under the category of "can do without". Ration stamps were issued to Americans. Ration books became a way of life for everyone at home during World War II. Each book was filled with ration stamps. You had to have ration stamps to buy things at the store. It still cost money, but you couldn't even buy an item unless you had stamps. The stamps were based on items that were in short supply and the number of people in the household. If you used up your stamps then you waited until the next issue before you could buy, that is, if it was still available, and you had the money. Many items we take little thought of today, were luxuries then. A lot of everyday things were in short supply. For instance, my older sister would help Mama mix a yellow salty powder in lard to make "margarine" for our bread and such, when butter was not available. We felt blessed when a neighbor who had a cow would sell folks milk and butter. Daddy paid for it by doing some work for her. Once this neighbor sold us the usual jug of milk, and upon inspection, Mama noticed bits of cornbread floating in the milk and surmised the milk was poured from glasses the farmer's children didn't finish. That ended our neighborhood's supply of dairy!

We had a modest garden and grew vegetables. Some years we had a pig. We had chickens that "free-ranged" in our yard providing us with eggs and an occasional Sunday dinner. Daddy brought home squirrel or rabbit after hunting during winter months. In the summer we had our fresh garden vegetables, and would go fishing down at the creek, catching supper and sometimes breakfast. The year we had a pig rendered wonderful pork chops ham and bacon. The pig was hung to cure from the rafters in the smoke house. The fat from the pig was boiled in a big black caldron in the back yard. This would render lard. Mama would let us drop potatoes in the lard as it bubbled and we had what now would be French fries--- but all together. Mama also made soap from the lard. This would be used year-round in the old wringer-type washing machine that sat on the back porch. In winter, clothes were washed, ran through the wringer, then dried by the fire or stove. In summer, we hung them outside on a clothes line. All but our socks and "seat covers" had to be ironed.

Baths were taken once a week in a large galvanized tub in the kitchen. Water was heated on the wood-stove. When young, we took baths together. As we grew, baths were taken by ourselves -- but in the same water. In the summer, we could take showers outside in a sort of "lean to" Daddy constructed with a huge metal drum on top that collected rain water. Mama made a curtain for the "doorway". It was often more convenient to take what Mama called a "Spitz Bath". This was using a basin and soapy water and as Mama put it ---"wash everything possible". She would shampoo our hair once a week.

We canned jars of fruits that we picked mostly from wild cherry, apple and persimmon trees. These were a great source for pies,,.. and sometimes worms! Some fruits were made into jam. Vegetables that we relied on in winter months were also canned. All other necessities were bought at Stout's Grocery Store. Mama would telephone an order and Mr. Stout would deliver them for us in his big station wagon that had wooden panels on the side. There was no refrigerator, but we had an icebox. Ice was delivered by the "ice man" (our name for him) at weekly intervals. My siblings and I would run to his ice truck on sweltering summer days and he would take out his long ice pick and chip off a chunk of the cool blue delight for each of us. What a treat!

Summers were so much fun! A neighbor black family owned a tobacco farm and kids were hired to work in the tobacco harvest. My sister was going on ten, I was going on eight. We would go to the farm at sun-up and work until supper time. Our job was to hand three tobacco leaves at a time to a worker who would string them on a tobacco stick. When the stick was full, it was hung in the barn to cure. At the end of the day, most of the ceiling of the barn was now green. After the curing process, the tobacco was packed to take and sell to the tobacco company where it was used to make cigarettes, snuff, and chewing tobacco. We loved the work as there were kids we knew who also were hired. The farmer's wife would cook a big lunch for all workers. That was the best part! We ate outside on picnic tables.

It was fun when we sometimes got to ride standing up behind the huge horse-drawn tobacco bin as tobacco was picked. Handling the tobacco, our hands would get what was called "tobacco gum" all over our fingers. This black sticky goop was nearly impossible to remove. A huge negative, if we were not watching, some of the boys who worked there would find and put a fat green tobacco worm down your shirt back and smack the shirt to squish it. Naturally, we did not take this silently! We were each paid fifty cents a day. Mama used the extra funds to buy our school supplies.

If I close my eyes and listen, I think I could still hear Mama's peddle sewing machine whirring late into the night as she sat sewing a dress, shirt or skirt one of us needed. Often as not, the cloth came from one of her own dresses that she had ripped apart, or fabric from feed sacks that had been cut open, washed and dyed with Rit dye. Her patterns were made from newspapers, and garments that fit were used as outlines. Sometimes Mama made our clothes out of real sold-by the-yard fabric, when available. Afterwards, every scrap was salvaged to be used in making a quilt. Her slogan was "waste not - want not", and "want" was most familiar at that time to families living in rural North Carolina.

Once I had a "new" dress and I proudly wore it to school. A girl in my class asked me where I had gotten it, and in my six-year-old innocence, I said, without embarrassment, "It came in a paper bag left on my porch!" I recall the puzzled look she had given me. You see, most of my clothes were passed down from my older sisters and most of their clothes were given to them by other families whose children had outgrown them. To us they were new, and we relished getting such gifts. These were not called "second-hand" or "hand-me-down" clothes, but instead we called them *"experienced"* clothes.

We were content during those times. I don't recall a whole lot of whining that things could be better, or complaints that we were "poor". We lived in a modest four-room-house, at the end of a long and dusty road that was framed by corn and tobacco fields. Indoor plumbing was rare in our part of the woods, so we never gave a second thought about using an outhouse, or drawing water from a well, as most folks did it that way.

I recall when we got our first telephone. It was a "party-line" with two other families. Too often, our phone would ring, and a "party-liner" would eaves a drop on our conversation. One of these was a paratrooper. When he was home, he would pick up our ring and heckle my older sister. Time would reveal that he finally met her, and history would record, they became man and wife, living to celebration of their 60th wedding anniversary.

My Daddy would say it was sinful to complain because there were a lot of families worse off than we were, and we should pray for them and count our blessings. His long discourses over meals reminded God how thankful we were to be rich and so blessed. With this in mind, I would of course say my prayers at night and include the poor children, whoever they were. It was in the sixth grade at school that I encountered my first rich kid. A girl named Edith. Her father was a truck driver who made runs from Florida to North Carolina hauling bananas, oranges and such. She wore pretty clothes and shoes she got to pick out herself. It was this rude awakening that made me realize that our family did not qualify for that title! These sparing traits of my parents though, certainly carried down through the family.

They each had completed only three grades in school, but encouraged us and listened to our lessons almost every night during the school year. They made sure we were doing our learning before we could hear our favorite serial shows on the radio. We loved the mystery shows, like "Inner Sanctum" or "Alfred Hitchcock". Westerns like "The Lone Ranger" were favorites of the whole family. Comedians, The Jack Benny Show" and "Ozzie and Harriet Show" were always a hit. They would put us kids rolling on the floor with laughter! These shows would follow the news. I remember one time my Daddy calling Mama in from the kitchen and telling her: "Hurry, come and sit-down, Winston Churchill is about to give a speech!" Then, there was Christmas and we wrote letters to Santa that were read on the radio. We would listen to hear our letter read.

The war ended, and times were somewhat kinder. My siblings and I grew up, left our humble beginnings, and began independent lives. Those life-lessons and values that were taught us when we were young, still remain with us. As we got older, the enduring wisdom they imparted seem to increase in value.

Just out of high school, I married a boy from "the other side of the tracks". His parents were well-to-do. He never ceased to be amazed at my sense of frugality. I recall once meeting him on the cellar stairs with a large box he was carrying to the trash. Of course, I had to rescue my two-dozen empty toilet tissue rolls, gift wrap from previous gifts that had been smoothed and folded among neatly wound balls of ribbon and twine, and bits and pieces of colorful paper destined to be cut into gift tags. There were other "keepers" in the box. As his bewildered face deadpanned, he reached into the box and held up two parts of what use to be a rather delicate and pretty china plate. Lowering his voice a notch while raising one eyebrow, he said to me, "Really?" I told him I was almost certain it could be rejoined and some good use could be made of it. He quietly held up one piece after another and watched in quandary as I smiled and nodded my head, carefully placing each unique item back in the box. Leaving him empty handed, I walked away muttering, "You never know when they will come in handy."

When our marriage ended in divorce, after twenty-three years, (not related to my penchant for saving stuff), I was left with four children to raise and educate without help. Times were hard as I eked out a living on a minimum wage job (to be exact, $1.20 an hour) with side jobs to boot.

Throughout their growing years, they somehow instinctively knew: if they had a need for a specific item, perhaps for a school assignment, and perchance it would be in the middle of the night when they would recall this was due in class the following day -- they would give a sigh of relief. They knew that somewhere it was tucked away and their mother could lay hands on it quicker than a wink!

Now, all my young ones are grown, have college degrees, married, and growing up children of their own. I would like to think that in their basement, attic or garage, there is a box of "might come in handy" stuff tucked away for what folks now call "a rainy day". Just yesterday, daughter number three, a kindergarten teacher, was stopping by to drop off her two-year-old twins I baby-sit for. She rushed inside exclaiming, "I forgot that today we are learning shapes and 1 need a block of wood this wide and this long for attaching my cut-outs" (making invisible measurements with her hands). Before she could catch her breath, I whisked myself downstairs to the basement, frantically stirred the dust on a few crates and boxes. I knew there must be something there that would fit the bill! Sure enough, I came up the steps holding what looked like an oversized somewhat smooth wooden brick. "Perfect", she said, smiling, as she dashed to her mini-van.

Jenny Bates

Velvet Bullies

I

I place the open books tenderly one,
top of the other, like honest lovers.
Words face words,
strip each other's meaning.
Shallots peeled of husk reveal
off-the-grid glow.
Cat stretches in moonlight,
stranding language.
Under the elephant,
the chipmunk dines.
Forest-old shadows sing:
the hawk is on the hunt today.
Longing cries in a cloudless sky.
Autumn is late, leaves keep
the hidden from the hunter.
Flinching meadow's edge pulses
like a river after a cool night.
Everything slants in frightened
animal retreat, wrinkled by
rain and cold.

New combinations of forest icons, patient,
clamoring about the purpose of change.

II

Clear, melodious Canta-lupo sits in shade,
composes poetic letters to friends
that cling to millennial terror.

Tiny deaf bear, no comfort among
craggy cliffs, deep woods,
path lined with stones.
If we met now, dear wolf,
I would forebear to interrupt
your poetry, fragmenting, decorating
this-little-place.

III

Under the burning Dog-star,
chatter and ripple of Bandusian spring.
Solace in its nacre hollows, mere quiet.
Ravens flutter their wings in warning —
　　　You must give it back!
Mushrooms umbrella your grave.
Still-shine, as a deer caught,
we soaked each other into light.
Lovers again.

Field notes full of velvet bullies:
　　　my hand hovers over a fresh track
　　　as big as my palm.

Mary Hennessy

Mexico City
Where Montezuma Expecting God
Got Cortez

1.

Because she wears a crown of iguanas
she looks like God,
first the corn

then the dark-eyed people of the corn.
She wears black trousers under
a cotton skirt, a care-

less beauty,
framed by stone arches built
by the Spanish.

Her inventory sits at the open-mouth of the metro
in a small pasteboard box
two packs of cigarettes,

three or four of chicle
and half dozen red jellied candies.
She is eating the inventory.

2.

Built by the Spanish, my ass—
the gringa watches.
Men like toreadors

with lines of silver buttons that flicker
insects
their silver wings in motion

up and down mariachi

legs that sing.
The gringa wants to dance

to the rhythm
of the tortilla machine
chilies, menudo y música.

She wants to hold a fan and wear a fedora
belly-button to belly-button in the metro—
no waist too wide.

The gringa wants DNA
from people who reach into your chest
and seize your beating heart.

Build a wall. Yes. Hair thick as night
and tamales on this side, corn
on the other.

Steve Cushman

Winning and Losing

Sometimes, after dinner,
my son and I play Gub, a silly
card game. He usually wins.
I'm fine with this. He's thirteen,
recently discovered privacy,
started locking his bedroom drawer.
So when he says *let's play*
and I'm tired and all I want to do is
grab a beer and settle into my
chair, stare at the TV for a few minutes
as I try to shake off the day,
I say *yes, of course, let's play*
He says *I'm going to win.*
While I don't say it out loud,
I think, Trevor, you already have.

Tina Egnoski

You Can Tell Me Anything

Matt left work early to pick up his daughter from her summer job. They had an hour ahead of them at the stable, grooming and feeding the horse, mucking the stall. If the heat loosened its mighty grip and Carly wanted to ride, closer to three hours. That was okay, Matt didn't mind. These days the stable was a refuge, the only place they spent time together without the shadow of that day she drove off to the West Bay Women's Clinic hanging between them.

J and C Farm was ten miles out of town, on a pitted dirt road. Matt clicked the A/C to max. It was early August and ninety-seven degrees, had been for five weeks. No rain, no relief. A punt of dust enveloped the car.

He parked and, without a word, Carly skipped off to join a group of kids standing about the soda machine. She hugged the two girls, as if she hadn't seen them in months, even though on Monday they had taken the horses to Battel Lake. The boy—that was who Carly really wanted to see. Jeans tucked into dusty boots, shirt unbuttoned in the heat, he had black hair, closely cropped, the way boys wore it these days, and dark eyes. He handed Carly his Coke and she took a sip, saliva mixing. Matt couldn't remember his name, but he seemed like an okay kid. Of course, Doug Feller, Carly's on-off boyfriend for the past two years, had once seemed like a nice boy. Boys, at first, sent her mood soaring. The free-fall came later.

Matt swept the tack room. Strips of gummy fly paper hung from the rafters. Though improbable, he was sure he smelled the rotting carcasses of insects. Next, he took a comb to Shasta's mane, yanking knots of hair. The horse was ornery, ragged. Sweat ran down her withers. Using his hand like a squeegee, he flicked it away. She hooved the fence rail, splitting off a piece of the decayed plank.

"Easy, girl," Matt said and yanked her halter.

Just then, Sam Kirkland came over and with crinkled brow said, "Looks like you got a sick horse there."

Matt agreed she hadn't been herself lately, but this heat made everybody, every *body*, brittle, just this side of mean.

Kirkland was the father of the two girls Carly rode with, twins, the same age as Carly, seventeen. He owned a spirited appaloosa and leased a bay from the stable owner. That was one way to cut costs. Matt often wondered why he and his ex-wife hadn't gone that route.

Now Peter Wynn sidled up next to Kirkland. He too had noticed Shasta's behavior. Hands in pockets, the stance of a relaxed expert, he told them about his own mare's bout of colic. The signs—flank biting, pawing, lack of appetite, the pitiable way the horse squatted, lifted her tail and strained—how had Matt missed it? Colic, he knew, could kill.

Beth Tepper joined them. What was this, an equine intervention? She had been his daughter's first riding instructor. She owned three quarter horses, beautiful beasts, stars of the local horse show circuit. Matt trusted her judgment.

"The only man to call is Frank Doyle," Beth said.

Dr. Doyle, a vet Matt knew only through word-of-mouth. He had yet to need him.

"Hopefully he can make it tonight," Beth said. "Mention my name."

Carly, beside him now, asked, "Hey, what's up?" She still held the boy's Coke.

"Looks like I have a long night ahead."

"You mean I can't ride?" she whined.

"Jesus, Carly," he said. "Can't you think of anyone but yourself?"

She turned her face into her hair, believing, still, the way she had as a girl, that hiding behind her bangs took her right out of the world. Invisible.

"Alright," she said. "I didn't know it was such a big deal."

Matt had been a fool to keep the horse after Liz left. Too much work, worry and expensive upkeep. He found it satisfying to heap everything on his ex: she had wanted out, she moved away, she was too busy reclaiming her twenties to take Carly on visitation weekends. Blame was hollow, though. To sell Shasta now, to lose her, would be the end.

He headed for the car for his cellphone. He needed to call the vet. Turning back to Carly, he said, "Give her some water, but no food."

He had no idea if this was the right thing to do.

When Carly was born, Matt decided he wanted to be an Involved Dad, a catch-phrase of the nineties. He did it all. Feed her, changed her diapers, bathed and powered her, snapped her into onesies, sang Bob Dylan as a lullaby. She was colicky, a real screamer. Walking, bouncing, pacifying, swinging—none of it quieted her. One night, in exasperation, arms aching, Liz stripped off the bed sheet and wrapped it around herself and Carly like a sling. Matt had seen mothers at the park with a similar store-bought contraption. He went the next day and purchased one. That was how they survived the next few months, with Carly, infant football, tucked under his or Liz's arm.

By age two, Carly had learned the power of camouflage. She hid behind walls, under tables and blankets, inside her T shirt, pulling arms and head in like a turtle. She used her long often-matted hair—she refused to let anyone cut or comb it—as a shield. Wry and broody, a secret keeper, she never talked about her days at school, from kindergarten on up. Report cards or notes from teachers somehow got lost. Once, a broken rib on the playground went untended for days, until she finally whimpered in pain. In junior high she didn't tell them she had been chosen for first chair, flute. He prompted her—they both did—holding out a coin, often a quarter, thinking both the bribe and the joke would amuse her: *Penny for your thoughts.* She would have none of it.

When scolded, she clammed up, clamped down. It drove them crazy. Liz stayed up late reading parenting books. They tried timeout, spanking, withdrawal of attention. Frustrated, they fell back on platitudes: *Look at me when I talk to you. What do you have to say for yourself? Go to your room until you're ready to talk.*

Later, after one of these scoldings, Matt would find Liz sitting on Carly's bed, pleading, "Please tell me. I'm your mother, you should be able to tell me anything." Carly appeared to be asleep, but Matt was pretty sure she was pretending. Advance, retreat: he couldn't keep up with those two. When Carly finally broke, months of grievance poured out along with tears and snot. In a stream of nonsensical babble, she gave a list of all their wrongs, all the ways they had ruined her life.

Over years of trial and error, Matt developed the ability to recognize subtle changes in his daughter's behavior. She would sit next to him unexpectedly while he watched television or she might show a sudden interest in his past. This was her way of letting him know she wanted to talk. He learned when to hang back and when to ask *Hey, sweetie, is everything okay?* If he approached too soon, he lost his chance. Too impatient for this method, Liz, more often than not, bit into Carly. Their relationship turned into was raw wound.

At ten, after reading *National Velvet*, Carly begged for riding lesson. Atop a horse, she transformed. Sulk to shine. She made friends with other horse-loving girls. She rode in shows and charmed the judges, won ribbons and trophies.

She was twelve, the age Liz said girls began to bend to societal pressure—be good, be polite, be pretty and dumb—when they purchased Shasta, an extravagant birthday gift. It was too much, Matt thought, but he didn't want to see this spark of joy extinguished, and he certainly didn't want to be the one to douse it.

Liz called her blissful. In that comment was envy. Seeing her daughter so fulfilled, so in love with something, reminded Liz what she had once wanted: to own and manage a restaurant. Matt realized this weeks later when Liz came to him with all her unhappiness. Motherhood, marriage, work as a distributor of restaurant equipment—it wasn't enough. She loved him and Carly, yes, but even *that* wasn't enough. This unburdening, similar to way their daughter handled her misery, caught him by surprise.

Liz moved to Crescent City to manage a seaside bistro. Carly chose to stay with Matt. Her mother's sudden change was confusing. Even Liz's promise of a new bedroom with new furniture she could pick out herself made no impact. Carly had no interest in starting over. She liked her bedroom, filled with every stuffed animal she had ever owned, a rock collection from when she was six and a poster she made when she ran for room monitor in the fourth grade. She wouldn't let Liz or Matt throw anything away. She liked routine.

After the divorce, Matt changed jobs, found a flexible, single-dad-friendly company that sold telecommunications systems. All day he wrote catchy promotional copy, dumbing down technospeak. After work, he and Carly went to the stable. They split the chores and after everything was done, she rode with the other kids, these days both girls and boys.

Matt enjoyed the activities of caring for Shasta, tasks with a purpose and a result that was satisfying—they eased the kinks in his shoulders and erased all the silly words in his mind. He also welcomed the camaraderie of the other horse owners. They sat together at the picnic table outside the paddock, talked of horse shows and feed and breeding. In these moments, he knew he had done the right thing, keeping Shasta, keeping the spark.

The vet arrived at a quarter-past eight. By then, everyone else had fed their animals, wished Matt luck and gone home. Kirkland, though, had returned with a sandwich and coffee. He offered to stick around and take a turn with the horse.

"Guess it's time for my initiation," Matt said, politely letting him off the hook.

Carly stayed by Shasta's side, stroking her neck. She whispered into her mane, but Matt couldn't hear what she said.

Doyle, a man of few words, worked quickly. Before Matt knew it, he had subdued the mare with a twitch and threaded the nasogastric tube down her right nostril.

"This'll do the trick," he said.

Instruments back in the satchel, Doyle shook Matt's hand and reminded him to keep Shasta moving. Crudely put, the horse had to shit before Matt could go home.

"That was fun," Carly said. "Now what?"

He gave her the car keys and told her to go on home, get some sleep. She obliged without protest. At the gate, she turned and waved.

They walked, horse and owner, pinched by physical exertion and humid air, circling the corral as finally, finally the sun set. Stable lights came on, humming, artificial moons that attracted and confused the insects. Navigational skills out of whack, blind and heedless, moths and beetles dive-bombed Matt.

Shasta whinnied, jerked against the halter. She wanted loose, she wanted to lie down and roll the fire out of her gut.

"Let's keep moving," he said.

At the crest of the barn, Matt picked out Venus right there under the moon, then scanned the sky for Mars. The summer Carly was five she developed a serious case of bedtime blues. She grumbled and stomped and kicked and by the time he got her in pajamas, she was an exhausted mess of tears and sweat. Liz had gone away for a week with some friends, her first real vacation since Carly's birth, so it was just the two of them. To break up the routine, Matt spread a blanket in the backyard, sprayed arms and legs with Off and made a game of counting stars. *One, two, three, four. Gazillion.* That was her favorite number. Matt pointed out the brightest stars: Sirius, Betelgeuse, the defining points of the Big Dipper. The word Betelgeuse—beetle juice—gave Carly the giggles. Daddy, you know everything in and out of the world, she said.

Matt held her and tickled her and threatened to find a fat beetle to squeeze and serve for breakfast. She wiggled and giggled until he had to let go, so she could run inside to the bathroom. He followed her and after a quick brush—she insisted on using nothing but a pink princess toothbrush—he coaxed her into bed.

When Liz returned, she balked at their new routine. She wanted no part of it, said Matt was giving in to Carly's histrionics. He didn't care and kept it up, with one condition, he explained that once Labor Day arrived, they had to go back to the old way. When the time came, Carly complied.

For several weeks in March of this year, Carly had been sulky. Well, sulkier than usual. She was just finishing her junior year, busy with exams and end-of-year parties, and Matt thought she might be overwhelmed. He waited, watched for a sign that let him know it was safe to ask. This time, though, after three days of near-complete silence—she answered any query with *yea* or *nah; hello* was a grunt and a nod—she came to him. Sunday morning, he stood at the counter trying to come up with a ten-letter word for mellow, gnawing the pencil eraser. Why did he even attempt the crossword? He was no good at it.

"Dad, I need you to sign a permission slip," she said.

What now? A last-minute field trip?

She slid the paper to him.

Planned Parenthood, Surgical and Sexual Health Services.

"Have a seat," he said and they moved to the table.

It all came out, the way it had when she was young. Doug was an ass, he said he loved her and he said he'd pull out and he said a girl couldn't get pregnant on the first time anyway and none of it was true. *Pull out*, that made Matt wince.

I have been notified that it is the intention of Planned Parenthood to provide abortion services for . . .

Matt had liked on-again, off-again Doug Feller. He was the antithesis of the shaggy-haired, shifty-eyed boys Matt saw loitering on the front steps at school, jockeying for position, scrutinizing girls. He noticed them on the mornings Carly missed the bus and he drove her to school. They were him, twenty-five years ago. Cocky and manipulative, boys who would say anything for a—what do they call it these days?—a hookup.

I understand that this form serves both as parental notification of and consent to abortion services to a minor by Florida law.

Since about ninth-grade, right after Liz moved out, Doug had been a part of Carly's life. At first, he was a friend who shared her interest in comic books and coin collecting. After they went to their first homecoming dance, it turned serious. But serious was easily replaced with *It's so over*, which in turn, weeks later, became *He's the best, Dad*. Last Matt knew they were off, for more than half the school year.

I waive the 48-hour notification requirement.

How were these things done? Should they go to family counseling? Should he see a minister? That was out of the question, they didn't belong to a church. Surely, before proceeding, he should meet with the boy's parents. He mentioned this last possibility and Carly shrieked.

"Oh God, no," she said. "Please, Dad, don't do that."

She had everything figured out. Doug knew and—not that it was required—he agreed with her decision. Neither of them was ready for a baby. Twice she had been to the clinic in Crosby to talk with a nurse about options, about how much her heart hurt. She showed him the brochures.

For the first time in years, he wished Liz was here. Always level-headed in a crisis, she would know the right thing to say, to do. But she wasn't here and right now Matt needed time to think it all through.

"Let's talk again tomorrow," he said.

Carly agreed. "I'm so sorry, Dad. I'm just so, so sorry." She wasn't crying, but she looked as if she might, any minute, break open.

He lifted her, hugged her. "It's okay," he said. "We'll get through this."

They spent the rest of the day at the stable. She stayed with him and they dispensed with their tasks in no time. Later that night, after Carly was in bed, he called Liz, fully intent on giving her the bad news. Before he could, she burst out with news of her own. Good news. The restaurant had received a five-star write up in the *Orlando Sentinel*. People were driving hours to eat at her place. He knew her eyes—pretty eyes, a hazel-brownish and almond-shaped— were shiny and flitting, the way they had when they first met and she talked for hours about her ambitions for the future—a future she was now in the midst of.

He couldn't tell her. It wasn't the right time. Would there ever be a right time? When he hung up, he remembered the night of Carly's birth. The nurse had told him to hold one of Liz's legs while she held the other. Every time Liz pushed, he and the nurse torqued his wife's legs to her ears. He would break a bone, he thought. But he didn't and then Carly's head appeared and her body slipped out and he cried and Liz cried and it was the best day.

Matt had been on his feet for twelve hours—it was nearly four in the morning. He and Shasta had circled the corral twelve hundred times, it seemed. His ankles throbbing. A makeshift table, barrel and plywood set up outside the tack room, held what was left of the thermos of coffee Kirkland had brought, probably cold and sour by now. Matt tied the reins and poured a cupful. Yes, it was cold, but sweet and good. He crouched, taking the pressure off his lower back.

Something nibbled at his ear. He struck, mechanically— damn mosquitoes—but his hand met the bristly lips of the horse and she bit him. Not hard, not enough to draw blood, but clearly she was suffering and wanted him to know it. He placed his cheek to her nose. Crazy, how he was drawn to this smooth, almost hairless spot: a shank of vulnerability. Earlier, when Frank Doyle had tightened the vice to keep her from jerking away, Matt was nauseous. Forehead to forelock, he whispered reassurance. *Come on girl, let it out. It's okay. I'm here.* If Shasta had a mind to, she could take a chunk out of his cheek.

A week after he made that phone call to Liz, he took the permission slip to the clinic to sign and have it witnessed. Out front, gathered about fifty-feet from the door—they weren't allowed to block the sidewalk or entryways—a small crowd of protesters held placards of slogans, scripture and enlarged pictures scrambled-egg fetuses. One woman was on her knees, praying inaudibly. God, Carly would have to walk right past them.

Inside, the woman behind the glass window was on the telephone. He noticed she had one of his company's systems, an old model, one designed especially for this size operation.

She put the call on hold and slid open the door with a *May I help you.*

He held up the piece of paper.

"Does your daughter have an appointment?" she asked.

"Yes, I believe so," he said.

"One moment, please." She closed the window and went back to the call.

The waiting room was packed with half a dozen teenage boys. Boyfriends. Or brothers. They sat on the plastic chairs, slumped, shaky-legged. Two girls shuffled out the door leading from the examination rooms. One was skinny, with a cropped top revealing a pierced bellybutton. The other had long stringy hair, similar to Carly's, only hers was held back at the sides with pink barrettes.

She would leave this place changed. They all would. They *did*. He was old enough, had enough distance and detachment from his past to know that some events lose their power, while others stick. Forever.

He and Carly had talked only once after she gave him the permission slip. What about adoption, he asked and her response was: *This just seems somehow, I don't know, cleaner.* Though logical, it sounded too clinical or maybe too much like an adolescent girl who didn't quite believe the whole thing was real and at the same time wanted to get it over with, a geometry test or a trip to the dentist.

He offered to take Carly to the appointment, for fatherly moral support, she was horrified by the suggestion.

"Just sign it, okay," she snapped, embarrassed for the first and only time. "It's bad enough I have to even do this."

"Then you should've kept your pants on," he said and regretted. Not the comment, but his fury and his timing. All that should come later, afterwards, when she was back to herself.

"I'm not that kind of girl," she said.

"I know," Matt said. "I'm sorry I said that." He sat on the bed next to her and she let him. She let him stroke the back of her head.

He tried then, to bring it up again. He could drop her off, wait in the car.

"No, Dad," she said. "Please. I just have to do this my way."

If he pushed, she'd sink back into silence and all would be lost. Their time together was running out. School would start again soon, Carly's senior year, her last year at home, and with it homework and band practice. She might keep the job, which meant Saturdays, the day they usually spent together at the stable, were gone.

In her typical way, Carly had treated this—her pregnancy and the abortion—like everything else. She stewed, then spewed, and in between she planned.

Finally the receptionist opened the window and asked for his driver's license. She typed several things into a computer. Thumb-tacked on the wall behind her was a Rosie the Riveter calendar. Yes, he told himself, we don't like it, but we can do it.

At dawn, Matt and Shasta were wiped out. The horse had finally released all her waste. When it came, it came in a sickening mess of oat and dirt and mineral oil. Matt could shrug off most anything—a night of no sleep, snorts and whinnies that were a kind of steady lament, teeth in the flesh of his palm—but the sight of such a regal animal hunkered and overwrought made Matt turn away.

He put Shasta in her stall. The air was rife with dust and approaching heat. The sun, just cresting the pines, gave him a whack over the head before disappearing behind a cloud. Maybe it would rain.

He heard an engine in the parking lot and saw Carly get out of the car. Holding up a bag of take out—probably a fried egg sandwich from Winton's, with some home fries if he was lucky—she smiled, looking so much like a young Liz. Her hair, pulled back in a ponytail, gave her face an open innocence. From this distance he couldn't see the freckles brought out each May by the sun, but he knew they were there. So were the quills of dark skin under her eyes, a sign of weariness.

In the end, Carly went to the clinic with her best friend Michelle. He waited at home, pacing, drinking cups of hot tea. He stripped the sheets from both beds, washed and replaced them. They smelled clean and fresh, like the lavender biodegradable detergent she insisted they use.

When she returned, she looked like those girls he had seen: tender, beaten-up, a shuffle walk, not necessarily because anything hurt but it might, at any moment, at the slightest misstep. As the days passed, he watched for any red flags of depression: lack of appetite and energy, insomnia, irritability. He scrutinized her face for signs of change. Had the experience given her a wrinkle of experience? She looked tired, but no different. He hoped that inside she was different, more cautious, more forgiving. Of herself.

That long ago summer when she was five and they watched the stars come out, Matt had explained how the planets orbit around the sun. Carly put her hands on her hips and refused to believe. The world revolved around her and don't try to convince her otherwise. Her body, making its way toward him now, still held a trace of that conceit—a naïve arrogance. It wasn't as cute on a seventeen-year-old, but it was effective. It was the way she faced a world that had spun out of her control.

She laughed at Matt. He must look a mess, as spent and rumpled as he felt. He hadn't lost her yet. They still had time. There was a year of calculus to get her through, and the SAT, a prerequisite she had thus far avoided. There would be homecoming and prom and maybe—most likely—boys. They'd get through it. There were the holidays, split per the custody agreement: this year Carly with him for Thanksgiving, with Liz for Christmas. Spring break hadn't been decided yet and that was okay.

If, in the coming months, he pushed her to talk more than

she wanted, it was okay. If he didn't push, okay. If she whined and he lost his temper, okay. If they argued about where she was going and with whom, okay. If they worked side-by-side at the stable with no words between them, okay. If, when he dropped her off at college, he heard in her good-bye a little-girl squeal of panic—*I'm not ready, Dad, not yet*—it was okay. He had done his best. They both had. It was okay.

Contributors

Cathy Adams: Cathy's latest novel, *A Body's Just as Dead*, was published by SFK Press. Her short stories have been published in *Utne, AE: The Canadian Science Fiction Review, Tincture, A River and Sound Review, Crack the Spine, Portland Review,* and over forty others internationally. She now lives and writes in Shenyang, China, with her husband, photographer, Julian J. Jackson.

Pamela Akins: Originally from Texas, Pamela Akins spends her winters in Sarasota, Florida, and summers in New London, Connecticut. Following an early career in publishing and marketing in the Northeast, she founded Akins Marketing & Design, an ad agency that served regional, national and international accounts for 28 years. Her work has been published in *A Letter Among Friends*, Best of Writers in Paradise journal Sabal, and Emerald Coast Review. Her short story *Rodeo Kisses* was selected as Flyway Journal's 2019 Sweet Corn Contest Fiction Winner. She is a Contributing Editor for the Florida Book Review (floridabookreview.net).

Susan Alff: Susan lives in Cary, works at Quail Ridge Books, and has resumed writing after a long drought. She has studied with poet Betty Adcock over several years and is part of a poetry writing group. She has published in Wraparound South.

Joan Barasovska: Joan grew up in Philadelphia and has lived in North Carolina for nearly sixteen years. She is an academic therapist in private practice, treating children with learning disabilities and emotional and behavioral challenges. Joan cohosts the Flyleaf Books Poetry Series in Chapel Hill and serves on the Board of the North Carolina Poetry Society. *Birthing Age*, from Finishing Line Press (2018), is her first book of poetry.

Sam Barbee: Sam's poems have appeared Poetry South, The NC Literary Review, Crucible, Asheville Poetry Review, The Southern

Poetry Anthology VII: North Carolina, Georgia Journal, Kakalak, and Pembroke Magazine, among others; plus on-line journals Vox Poetica, Sky Island Journal, Courtland Review and The Blue Hour. His second poetry collection, *That Rain We Needed* (2016, Press 53), was a nominee for the Roanoke-Chowan Award as one of North Carolina's best poetry collections of 2016. He was awarded an "Emerging Artist's Grant" from the Winston-Salem Arts Council to publish his first collection <u>Changes of Venue</u> (Mount Olive Press); has been a featured poet on the North Carolina Public Radio Station WFDD; received the 59th Poet Laureate Award from the North Carolina Poetry Society for his poem "The Blood Watch"; and is a Pushcart nominee.

Jenny Bates: Jenny is a poet from the foothills of North Carolina and a member of Winston-Salem Writers and the NC Poetry Society. She has two published books, *Opening Doors: an equilog of poetry about Donkeys* (Lulu Publishing, Raleigh, NC); and *Coyote with Coffee*, a single poem fine craft volume (Catbird on the Yadkin Press, Tobaccoville, NC). Her work has been published in Flying South, Wild Goose Poetry Review, and Old Mountain Press. She is a consecutive contributing poet in Poetry in Plain Sight and in 2017 she was a top 10 Finalist in the Press 53 Single Poem Contest. Jenny's poetry has appeared in laJoie 2017- 2019, a quarterly publication of Animals' Peace Garden, dedicated to promoting appreciation for all beings. In 2019 her poem *Fame Looks Both Ways* was included in the Walt Whitman Bicentennial Celebration for publication in *Poets to Come*. Her new manuscript entitled, *Visitations* is due for publication in summer of 2019 (*Hermit Feathers Press*). Jenny currently volunteers as animal whisperer and helping hand at Plum Granny Farm. An organic local farm in Stokes County, North Carolina.

Teyako Bolden: Teyako is a recent graduate of Trident Technical College. She lives in Summerville, South Carolina and has enjoyed writing for as long as she can remember. She is a mom to two amazing little girls. Her daughters can always find her curled up with a good book.

Katherine Burnette: Katherine received her B.A. and J.D. degrees from Wake Forest University and has practiced law for almost 35 years. Her poems appeared in the Wake Forest Literary magazine and she was editor of The Jurist. In January, 2019, she received her MFA degree in Creative Writing, Fiction, from Queens University of Charlotte. She was appointed to the North Carolina state district court and serves in Franklin, Granville, Person, Vance, and Warren counties. She lives in Oxford, North Carolina with her husband, two parakeets her daughter left when she headed to graduate school, and a number of cats.

Courtney Lynn Camden: Courtney is a D.C. based writer whose work was most recently featured in Flying South (2017), Chaleur Magazine (May 2018), The Esthetic Apostle (August 2018), Cathexis Northwest Press (November 2018), and Junto Magazine (December 2018). She is overjoyed to once again join the Flying South family, and would like to thank above all else her ever-present parents and best friend Kelly Bryant. I love you all 3000. You can find more of her essays, poems, and pop-culture pieces here, at lynncam.com

Robyn Campbell: Robyn is a children's poet, picture book writer, and young adult novelist. Her poetry is published in over 15 venues. She's a member of Winston-Salem Writers, and the coordinator for their kid lit critique group, Magic Page. Robyn is a published and listed member of the SCBWI, and she'll be giving her workshop on voice in Charlotte NC at the SCBWI Carolinas conference on September 28th, 2019.

Paloma A. Capanna: Paloma is a writer and a proprietor of an antiques shop & used bookstore in historic Beaufort, NC. Most recently, she won a Second Place in Short Stories for *Citizens United* and a Second Place in Poetry for *Hurricane Florence - 2018* in the 2019 Carteret Writers Contest. She is a Board Member at Large for this local writers' group. She also recently presented at the Pamlico Writers Group conference on the topic of giving voice to the voiceless. She is a member also of this group. Her background is as a litigation attorney for more than 25 years, including work on civil rights cases these past seven years.

Joyce Compton Brown: Joyce has published in numerous journals, Her chapbooks are *Bequest* (Finishing Line Press, 2015) and *Singing with Jarred Edges* (Main Street Rag Publishing, 2018).

Steve Cushman: Steve has published three novels. His debut poetry collection, *How Birds Fly*, is the winner of the 2018 Lena Shull Book Award.

David Dixon: David is a physician, poet, and musician who lives and practices in the foothills of North Carolina. His poetry has appeared in Rock & Sling, The Northern Virginia Review, Connecticut River Review, FlyingSouth 2018, Sand Hills Literary Review, and elsewhere.

Joanne Durham: Joanne is a retired teacher, literacy supervisor and consultant who is lucky to live in Kure Beach, NC. She writes poetry for children and adults. Her work has been published by Pinesong, Flying South, and Poetry in Plain Sight, as well as in national teaching journals.

Meli Broderick Eaton: Meli grew up in Oregon and lived in multiple countries and on both coasts before settling back in her hometown. As a student at Sweet Briar College in Virginia, she studied in small workshops and one-on-one independent studies with poet Mary Oliver and author John Gregory Brown. Her poem *Stream* won 3rd place in the late 2017 The Source Weekly/OSU-Cascades MFA poetry contest out of nearly 300 entries. A group of her poems placed in the top 10 of 300 entries in a peer-judged contest and appear in Sixfold magazine's Winter 2019 issue. Her poem *Black Bird Blue* received honorable mention and came out in

Crosswinds Poetry Journal in May 2019. Her poem *Falling Stars* just won first place in the Oregon Poetry Association New Poets spring 2019 contest and will be published in the Verseweavers anthology early next year. She lives with her family on a suburban microfarm in Oregon and will begin an MFA program this summer.

Tina Egnoski: Tina is the author of several books, including the novella *In the Time of the Feast of Flowers*, winner of the Clay Reynolds Prize. Her work, both fiction and poetry, has been published in Carolina Quarterly, The Masters Review and Saw Palm Journal, among others. Her novel, *Burn Down This World*, is forthcoming from Adelaide Books. A Florida native, she currently lives in Rhode Island.

Michael Gaspeny: Michael's third chapbook, *The Tyranny of Questions*, will appear from Unicorn Press next spring. A novel in verse, it dramatizes a suburban mother's fight to overcome her demons in the 1960s. Gaspeny's previous chapbooks are *Re-Write Men* and *Vocation*. He has won the Randall Jarrell Poetry Competition and the O. Henry Festival Short Story Contest. For hospice service, he has received the North Carolina Governor's Award for Volunteer Excellence.

Jonathan Greenhause: Jonathan was the winner of both Aesthetica Magazine's 2018 Creative Writing Award in Poetry and the 2017 Ledbury Poetry Competition, a runner up in America's 2019 Foley Poetry contest, first runner-up in the 2018 Julia Darling Memorial Poetry Prize, a recipient of 2nd Prize in Cannon Poets' 2018 Sonnet or Not Poetry Prize, and a recipient of 3rd Prize in the Cornwall Contemporary Poetry Festival's 2018 Competition. His poems have recently appeared or are forthcoming in Columbia Poetry Review, Moon City Review, New Ohio Review, Redactions, and Salamander, among others. He was also a contributor to the last two issues of Flying South.

Chase Harker: Chase is a 21-year-old writer who attends UNCW.

Janis Harrington: Janis' book, *Waiting for the Hurricane*, won the 2017 Lena M. Shull Book Contest given by the North Carolina Poetry Society, and was published by St. Andrews University Press. Her poems have appeared in journals and anthologies in the USA and Europe, including: Beyond Forgetting: Poetry and Prose about Alzheimer's Disease, The Kent State University Press; New Southerner Anthology; The Homestead Review; Flying South; and Kakalak 2016 and 2018. Visit her at: janisharrington.com.

John Haugh: John lives in Greensboro, NC where he works in finance and is trying to assemble his first chapbook, *Repurposed Ghost Mixtape*. Recent other publishing credits include poems appearing in Main Street Rag, Kackalack, the Roanoke Review, Peregrine, Poetry in Plain Sight, and The Tipton Poetry Review. Mr. Haugh has won poetry awards, was a NCAA national champion in fencing years ago, and spent untold hours browsing Oxford Books in Atlanta and Powell's City of Books in Oregon when young.

Mary Hennessy: Mary was a nurse most of her adult life. She returned to school late and fell in with a community of generous, word-crazed people. Her poems have appeared in many journals and anthologies. One was nominated for a Pushcart Prize and included in the play *Deployed*. One rode the R-bus line in Raleigh. Poetry is the only thing that makes sense to her anymore.

Jo Ann Steger Hoffman: Jo Ann's publications include a children's book, short fiction and numerous poems in literary journals, including The Merton Quarterly, Persimmon Tree, Pinesong, Ground Fresh Thursday and Flying South, among others. She has received contest awards from the Carteret Writers, Pamlico Writers and the Palm Beach Poetry Festival. Her 2010 non-fiction book, *Angels Wear Black*, recounts the only technology executive kidnapping to occur in California's Silicon Valley. A native of Toledo, Ohio, she and her husband now live in Cary and Beaufort, North Carolina.

Allison Hong Merrill: Allison was born and raised in Taiwan and immigrated to the U.S. at age twenty-two. She is an author in both Chinese and English. Her essays won Grand Prize in the 2019 MAST People of Earth writing contest, first place in the 2019 Segullah Journal writing contest, third place in the 2015 Storymakers Conference First Chapter contest, Honorable Mention in the 79th Annual Writer's Digest Writing Contest in the Memoir/Personal Essay category. She was the finalist of 2014 Serendipity Memoir Discovery Contest. Her personal work can be found in the Life Story Anthology (Taipei, Taiwan), the Ensign Magazine, the Liahona Magazine, the LDS Beta Reader Mind Game Anthology, and Medium. She earned an MFA in Writing from Vermont College of Fine Arts. She is a member of the Utah Valley Writer's Group, and a committee member of the 2019 Storymakers Conference.

Glenna Hurlbert: Glenna loves to condense events of lives or the textures of our planet, great or small, into a few story-telling words. Her poetry has been collected in a number of anthologies such as those of: The Poetry Council of North Carolina; The Burlington Writers Club; Duke University Medical Center; The International Library of Poetry; The North Carolina Poetry Society. She has read at a number of sponsored readings, two of which are: The West End Poetry Festival in Carrboro, NC; Listen to Your Mother, William Peace University.

Alison Jennings: Alisonis retired from teaching and accounting; throughout her life, she has composed over 450 poems, and recently published several of them, in print journals and online. She lives in Seattle, where she writes poetry whenever she has time.

Don Johnson: Don has had a life long interest in the nature of peoples' assumptions, accurate and not. *The Bug* was intended to help people ponder our relations with the life around us. Don has a BS in Philosophy from Carroll College, 1956, an MBA from Northwestern University, 1970, and an MSW from The Ohio State

University, 2001. He enjoys writing, mostly for his own satisfaction, and has found an interested audience in the graduate school at Wake Forest University in Winston Salem.

Janet Joyner: Janet's prize-winning poems have been honored in the 2011 Yearbook of the South Carolina Poetry Society, Bay Leaves of the North Carolina Poetry Council in 2010, 2011, Flying South in 2014, and in 2015, as well as anthologized in The Southern Poetry Anthology, volume vii, North Carolina, and Second Spring 2016, 2017, 2018. Her first collection of poems, *Waterborne*, is the winner of the Holland Prize and was published by Logan House in February, 2016. Her chapbook, *Yellow*, was published by Finishing Line Press in November, 2018. *Wahee Neck*, her third collection, will be published next fall by Hermit Feathers Press.

Jeanne Julian: Jeanne is the author of two chapbooks: *Blossom and Loss* (Longleaf Press), and *Relic and Myth* (Prolific Press). Her full-length collection is forthcoming from The Poetry Box Select. Her poems appear in Prairie Wolf Press Review, Poetry Quarterly, Lascaux Prize 2016 Anthology, pacificREVIEW, and other journals, and have won awards from The Comstock Review, Naugatuck River Review, and The North Carolina Poetry Society, which awarded her with a 2018 Susan Laughter Meyers Poetry Fellowship honorable mention. www.jeannejulian.com

Bonnie Larson Staiger: Bonnie is an Associate Poet Laureate for North Dakota, the inaugural recipient of the 'Voices of the Plains and Prairies Poetry Award' (NDSU Press) for her debut collection, *Destiny Manifested*. She often writes of the poignant subtleties of life from the view of the high plains of the New American West as well as the many places she has traveled.

Jessica Lindberg: Jessica teaches at Georgia Highlands College, a community college in the northwest corner of the state. She earned her PhD from Georgia State University. A recipient of the Virginia Spencer Carr fellowship and the Mary Ann Brown Award, her poems have been published in various literary magazines and journals, such as the Mississippi Review, Glassworks, Third Wednesday, and others.

Donna Love Wallace: Donna Love Wallace of Lewisville, North Carolina, received a Wildacres Artist Residency to complete her first book of poetry titled Between the Stones (Hermit Feathers Press, forthcoming summer 2019). Donna has served in Winston Salem Writers and Poetry in Plain Sight. Her poetry appears in Pinesong and Snapdragon, among others.

Barbara Rizza Mellin (cover artist): Barbara is an award winning writer and artist (painter and printmaker), who relocated to Winston Salem from the Boston area, where she taught art for more than 30 years. Her artwork has been featured in juried exhibits and one-woman shows throughout the U.S and internationally online. Her art work has appeared on the covers and inner pages of Flying South, Kakalak, Liminal, and Willard and Maine literary magazines. She holds a graduate degree in Art History from Harvard, where she received the First Place *Crite Prize* for her thesis on the American artist Frank Vincent DuMond and is currently working on a book about that artist. She also writes frequently about the arts for national and local publications, including a bi-monthly column for Renaissance magazine.

Jesse Millner: Jesse's poems and prose have appeared most recently in Steam Ticket, The Split Rock Review, The Comstock Review, The South Florida Poetry Journal, and The West Texas Literary Review. Jesse teaches writing courses at Florida Gulf Coast University in Fort Myers, Florida.

Catherine Moore: Catherine is the author of three chapbooks, the poetry collection *ULLA! ULLA!*, and *FIOLET & WING: An Anthology of Domestic Fabulist Poetry*. Her work appears in Tahoma Literary Review, Southampton Review, Mid-American Review, Broad River Review and in various anthologies. She's been awarded Walker

Percy and Hambidge fellowships; her honors also include the Yemassee Fiction Prize, the Southeast Review's Poetry Prize, as well as Pushcart Prize, the Best of the Net, and VERA Award nominations. Her fiction has shortlisted in several competitions and was selected for inclusion in the juried BEST SMALL FICTIONS. Catherine holds a Master of Fine Arts in creative writing and she teaches at a community college. Her upcoming collection of lyrical pieces in the voices of bog bodies is forthcoming from Unsolicited Press.

Michael J. O'Connor: Michael is a writer and musician from California. He has worked as prose editor on the literary magazine, Zaum, and is a contributing writer for the satirical music blog, The Hard Times, as well as other publications.

Bradford Philen: Bradford writes and teaches high school English in the Philippines where he lives with his wife, two kids, and dog Bear. He holds an MFA from the University of Alaska Anchorage and has authored two books of fiction (*Autumn Falls*, 2011; *Everything is Insha'Allah*, 2014). His full list of publications can be found at https://bradfordphilen.com.

David E. Poston: David 's work has appeared recently or is forthcoming in Pedestal Magazine, Crack the Spine, The Cape Rock, Rise Up Review, Main Street Rag, and Atlanta Review. He is the author of three poetry collections: *My Father Reading Greek, Postmodern Bourgeois Poetaster Blues* (winner of the N.C. Writers' Network's Randall Jarrell/Harperprints Chapbook Award) and *Slow of Study*. He is a co-editor of Kakalak.

Helen Rossiter: Helen lives in Ottawa, Canada. Fiction awards include winner of the Alice Munro Short Story contest, winner of the Canadian Authors Association short story contest and second place in On The Premises. Her fiction has appeared in The Furious Gazelle, Avatar Review, Club House Press and others.

Joyce Schmid: Joyce's poetry has appeared in previous issues of Flying South, as well as Poetry Daily, Missouri Review, New Ohio Review, Antioch Review, and other journals and anthologies. She lives in Palo Alto, California, with her husband of over half a century.

Claire Scott: Claire is an award winning poet who has received multiple Pushcart Prize nominations. Her work has been accepted by the Atlanta Review, Bellevue Literary Review, New Ohio Review, Enizagam and Healing Muse among others. Claire is the author of *Waiting to be Called* and *Until I Couldn't*. She is the co-author of *Unfolding in Light: A Sisters' Journey in Photography and Poetry*.

Trish Sheppard: A few of Trish's publishing credits include: Kyso Flash, Kakalac, Shoal Journal. Awards include: Finalist Poet Laureate Competition NC Poetry Society, Finalist Palm Beach Ekphrastic Poetry Contest 2019, Honorable Mention Bank of the Arts Ekphrastic Contest 2018. She serves as a co-host for two critique groups in Carteret County NC.

Patricia J Slaga: Patricia is an 80 yr old writer. She has four children, who have made her grandmother to nine. She was first published in 1953 at the age of 13 in North Carolina Wildlife magazine, a poem: *What Rip Van Winkle Saw*. In 1985 she won first place in NC Mothers Association Literary Competition for a poem: *She Wanted You To See*. In 2005 she won North Carolina's Writers Workshop for *Unconventional Love* published in Flying South 2016. *For Love of a Dog* was published in Journey from Heartbreak to Hope in 2015 by Elizabeth G. Danielson. *When Tulips Bloom* was published in Flying South 2017. *Peace in the Storm* was published 2018, in Heart & Hand Quarterly Newsletter, of the Spiritual Care Support Ministries. She has been married 24 years to Paul Slaga, Vice President at a local bank. She retired from WS/FCS in 1999.

Robert Stewart: Robert is a published author with a new book to be released on Yeats, colonialism, religion, and the poetic possibilities of the post-colonial. He is originally from Ireland but lives in Virginia. He continues to travel extensively and regularly throughout the world.

Dawn Terpstra: Dawn's love of culture, magic and nature is a theme in her works. Her poetry appears in Lyrical Iowa, Haiku Journal, Cathexis Northwest Press, Meat for Tea: The Valley Review and forthcoming editions of High Shelf Press, and Lyrical Iowa (2019). She and her husband live in Iowa where she leads a communications team.

Emily Jon Tobias: Emily lives on the coast of Southern California while pursuing her MFA degree at Pacific University Oregon. She graduated from the University of Wisconsin Milwaukee in 2017 where she obtained her bachelor's degree in creative writing.

Lucinda Trew: Lucinda lives and writes in Charlotte, N.C. She studied journalism and English at the University of North Carolina at Chapel Hill and is an award-winning speechwriter. Her poetry and nonfiction work have been published or are forthcoming in The Fredricksburg Literary and Art Review, Mulberry Fork Review, Pinesong, High Shelf Press, The Dead Mule School of Southern Literature, Medium, The Mighty, Charlotte Viewpoint, BluntMoms, Boomer Café and Vital Speeches of the Day. She is a recipient of a 2019 North Carolina Poetry Society Award.

Emily Wilmer: Emily is a spiritual director, retreat leader, poet, co-director of Oasis of Wisdom: Institute for Contemplative Study, Practice and Living (www.oasisofwisdom.net) in Asheville, NC. Her poems have appeared in KAKALAK, Sufi Journal (UK), Thomas Merton Poetry of the Sacred finalist, Great Smokies Review, NC Poetry Society Poetry of Courage award winner, and various other journals.

Katherine Wolfe: Katherine lives in Goldsboro, North Carolina. She is a retired media coordinator with Wayne County Public Schools and a member of the Goldsboro Writers Group. Published works include the memoir *Savannah on My Mind* written with Bettye Clary Toomey and poetry in the Lyricist, Renaissance, Shoal, Pinesong, Flying South 2017, 2018 and the Winston Salem Writers series Poetry in Plain Sight. Her chapbook Time That Has Gone was published by Finishing Line Press in 2018.